HURRAH FOR GIN

HURRAH FOR GIN

A BOOK FOR PERFECTLY IMPERFECT PARENTS

KATIE KIRBY

CORONET

First published in Great Britain in 2016 by Coronet
An imprint of Hodder & Stoughton
An Hachette UK company

6

A CIP catalogue record for this title is
available from the British Library

Hardback ISBN: 978 1 473 63960 7
Ebook ISBN: 978 1 473 63959 1

Typeset in Consolas by Hewer Text UK Ltd, Edinburgh

Printed and bound by Clays Ltd, St Ives plc

Hodder & Stoughton policy is to use papers that are natural, renewable
and recyclable products and made from wood grown in sustainable
forests. The logging and manufacturing processes are expected to
conform to the environmental regulations of the country of origin.

Hodder & Stoughton Ltd
Carmelite House
50 Victoria Embankment
London EC4Y 0DZ

www.hodder.co.uk

CONTENTS

FOR IMPERFECT PARENTS EVERYWHERE

The ones who shout too much and silently scream fuck off into the fridge. The ones who have zero patience, dread playing tea parties and drink quite a lot of wine. The ones who forget permission slips and serve up beige freezer food for dinner (again). The ones who have library books well overdue and would be lost without biscuit-related bribery. The ones who are looking at their phones because sometimes it all just seems so mind-numbingly boring and the ones who sometimes dream about escaping but in reality couldn't be happy anywhere else but home.

This is for the parents who doubt themselves occasionally, often or always, when they really don't need to. Because to the only ones who truly matter, you are everything, and they couldn't possibly love you more.

TO ME, YOU ARE PERFECT

WHAT IS THE POINT OF THIS BOOK?

Hello my name is Katie and this is my book, I kind of hate writing introductions because I imagine people cringing when they read them but please bear with me I hope it will get better.

This is my family . . .

Actually, sorry, that's the one that I use as my screensaver to give people the impression we are capable of stuff. This one probably provides a more realistic view . . .

We are not (entirely) dysfunctional, we are (usually) pretty happy but we (sometimes) piss each other off. It's just the way it goes.

Big Bro is currently six and Little Bro is currently three, although a lot of this book is about when they were toddlers and babies because it's all about our journey as a family. I'm not writing it to tell you how it should be done (I don't actually know), I'm just sharing our stories in the hope that some of them might make you feel less like you're the only one messing things up.

You see I love my children, I REALLY love them, but I still find it fucking annoying when the littlest one empties an entire box of cereal out on the floor for fun, or when the biggest one is still pootling about in his socks after I've asked him 137 times to get his bloody shoes on.

That doesn't make me love them any less, it just means I need to drink more gin.

Also, here is a little upfront warning . . .

THIS BOOK CONTAINS SARCASM!

I hate having to spell that out but unfortunately there are a lot of people out there who cannot detect jokes and/or enjoy getting offended by inconsequential stuff.

Come on people – we all know children are a gift! It's just that they are a bit like a very expensive gift that all of your family chipped in to get you as a surprise; an over-the-top, gaudy bracelet that you will have to wear in public every day even though you're not sure you like it very much (that's sarcasm by the way).

When you sit with the wrapping paper open in your lap and everyone's looking expectantly for your reaction, you have no choice but to say . . .

. . . although you know it won't go with your favourite shimmery top that you like to wear to cocktail bars on Friday evenings. But you put it on immediately and you can't ever take it off in case you appear ungrateful.

There is no gift receipt.

One day you are out at lunch with a friend and after a couple of glasses of wine you say, 'Do you know what, sometimes I look at this bracelet and I just think URGH!' Instead of being shocked, your friend smiles and rolls up her sleeve. She's wearing a very similar bracelet. Suddenly you're both talking about how annoying it can be to wear this bracelet day in and day out, how its heaviness can weigh you down and how sometimes other people look at it, shake their heads and sigh (FYI you can diss your own bracelet but it's NEVER OK to diss anyone else's).

You look around the restaurant and see a lot of people out there struggling to coordinate their bracelets with their outfit choices. Some are fucking it up even worse than you, they look ridiculous but they're still laughing. So you laugh too. You start to feel normal.

And that bracelet, though it's busy, noisy and bright, maybe it's starting to suit you after all. When the sun catches it, at the right angle it looks like the most beautiful thing you have ever seen. It slipped from your wrist once, in the park, and you were gripped with fear that you might ever lose it. For it was chosen especially for you, it was delivered with love and now you realise how bare, how empty, your arms would feel without it.

P.S. To make extra sure we're all on the same page . . . In that bit above I was comparing having a baby to getting presented with a hideous bracelet on your birthday. That's called an analogy. You're welcome.

P.P.S. There's quite a bit of bad language in this book. I'd apologise in advance but we all know that swearing is big, it is clever and it is funny.

P.P.P.S. eBaying kids is not only morally wrong but also illegal.

GROWING A HUMAN

There are two types of pregnant people in this world, I have illustrated the differences in the scientific diagram above. Depiction A denotes the irritatingly healthy-looking ones and Depiction B denotes those who look like they are about to keel over and die.

Me? I was a B (yay).

Even now when people say to me 'Oh I didn't get morning sickness', I feel like grabbing a handful of their cheek and saying 'Well good for you!' while squeezing ever so slightly too hard.

Nausea for me is worse than pain and I quickly learnt that morning sickness isn't really morning sickness at all but unwavering, all-day, all-consuming sickness.

I also fell into the category of those who suffer from morning sickness, but aren't actually sick. The ones who are constantly gagging but with no follow-through. It's a strange one to deal with because on the one hand if you aren't actually going to vomit there is no need to keep running off to the toilet every few minutes. But on the other hand, dry-retching in front of other people is not exactly the most attractive thing to do. I could often be found hiding behind an item of furniture or well-placed piece of vegetation in my early weeks.

The only way to manage the nausea was to eat, eat and then eat some more. I could never allow myself to be anywhere near hungry because then the nausea would descend with gusto. My pockets were always full of sweets and biscuits that I would stuff into my gob when no one was looking, for fear they would clock my increasingly erratic behaviour.

Because chain-eating Hobnobs in a bush while resembling a corpse doesn't look at all suspicious, right?

I mean how are you meant to keep pregnancy a secret – how?! Another horrendous thing to deal with is social occasions because you will need to swerve alcohol. I guess it's fine if you are one of those people who often drives for convenience or does that healthy lifestyle shit; but what if you are one of those people who orders a round of Jägerbombs before suggesting karaoke because they totally forgot that they are not a teenager any more?

I'm not saying that person is me, but it might be me.

If you are one of those embarrassing drunks (or 'people who like to have fun' as I call them) then it becomes a bit more difficult to hide but it's not impossible. I got through my thirtieth birthday in the early stages of pregnancy without anyone cottoning on, with the help of a trusty friend in the know. You can swap glasses, order cranberry juice and pretend it's got vodka in or pour your drink away while you are in the loo. Sacrilege I know but desperate times . . .

And to be honest, going to the pub when you *have* revealed your pregnancy to the masses isn't much easier . . .

All in all I found that the first trimester properly sucked (obviously excluding the wonder of making a new person, etc.). Pregnancy books suggested I should have gained two to four pounds but due to the constant commitment to eating entire packets of biscuits in one sitting I now more accurately resembled a walking toilet roll with limbs.

The tubular stage

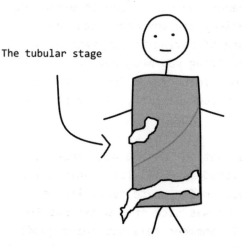

At this point you would give anything to be displaying a cute little bump but instead you clock people looking at you funny, wondering if you've just let yourself go a little. You might find yourself randomly shouting 'I'M PREGNANT YOU ARSEHOLE!' at the guy from accounts because he dared to glance up from his spreadsheet as you walked by.

Slowly the hairbands you were using to expand your jeans are insufficient and you move into the exciting territory of having to buy maternity clothes, if by exciting you mean paying loads of money for items of clothing you don't even like that will make you look slightly less shit than you do already.

The good news is that the nausea will hopefully subside and the tiredness will lift (unless you are one of the poor unfortunate souls like my sister Caroline who was sick from weeks five to forty). Anyway, I remember this bit being good! Little bubbles, little kicks and a little bump. A little smile on my face that was hard to wipe off.

That glow, that mystical glow they speak of, could I see it in the mirror? Could I finally cut back on the tinted moisturiser that was masking my dead look?

YES!

It lasted about three days and then I started to resemble a sea mammal.

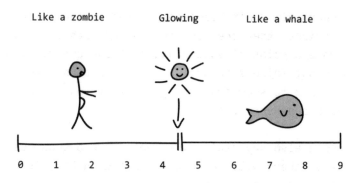

In the whale stage the baby grows bigger and those cute little flutters turn into whole limbs sliding visibly across your abdomen. Should you feel amazed or horrified? It's all so confusing.

You need to wee ALL THE TIME. You plan entire days around wee stops.

You have the same conversations with people over and over and over again.

Do you know what you are having? No.

Have you decided on a name? No.

Are you all prepared? No idea.

I certainly don't blame people for asking these questions, they are just interested right? In fact I make a point of asking all of these questions to pregnant friends in quick succession each time I see them to show just how goddam interested in their pregnancy I am.

People also say stuff like 'Well have a good rest now as there will be none of that when baby is here!' and then laugh.

Another one they like to say is 'Still not had the baby yet then?' To your face. While you are still obviously, massively pregnant.

The most popular thing people say is 'Wow your bump is massive/really small!' With absolutely no regard for how terrifying that is for a heavily pregnant person to hear.

You should pinch all of these people hard on the cheek also.

Unsolicited bump-fondling should be met with a kick to the shins.

Towards the end of your pregnancy you will suddenly notice you have started shuffling around like an old man. You can't put your shoes on. Everything aches. You can't see your fanny, you attempt to prune it blindly, you have no idea what a mess you have made and you don't even care.

The final few weeks are best reserved for lolling about on the sofa watching box sets, crying at the sight of your swollen sausage legs and swigging Gaviscon from a bottle like it's gin. (Oh gin, it won't be long!)

You will also do a thing you swore you'd never do called nesting. Kind of nice but also kind of full of rage. For example, you might find that the colour your sitting room is painted suddenly and inexplicably makes you want to kill your husband.

Relax. As a heavily pregnant person it is your basic human right to be totally unreasonable.

You might also get a strange panicky feeling a bit like the one you get at Christmas because the supermarkets are shut for like one day. The shops don't even shut when you have a baby but it feels like you must buy everything on every single baby list you can get your mitts on because it's perfectly possible that at 3:37 a.m. you might urgently need a baby bath thermometer right?

People will tell you you don't REALLY need all that stuff but you won't believe them. It is only about a year later, when you look at the huge piles of crap you have amassed, that you will realise how unhinged you were acting.

The last few days should be spent passive-aggressively replying to well-meaning texts. It's fine as long as you always, always remember to add the safety wink at the end.

Another thing to note is that the more natural labour-inducing remedies you try the longer your baby will take to come out.

They add +2 days for each cup of rancid raspberry leaf tea you drink. Fact.

The next time you get pregnant, if you are lucky (and brave) enough to do it again, you will probably notice that people don't really care. You've had your share of nice and now it's just boring for everyone. No one will offer to carry things for you, there will be zero resting and maternity leave will mean jack shit if you add a toddler into the mix.

The list of pregnancy moans and gripes could go on and on huh? You feel sick, you can't drink, you can't sleep, you can't wear normal clothes, you worry continuously, you wee continuously . . .

But all of that for me was sufferable ten times over, because ultimately pregnancy was a true privilege.

And it doesn't get more magic than that.

SOMETIMES YOU HAVE TO SAY GOODBYE

It's easy to look at pregnant women and seemingly perfect nuclear families and think, 'Wow, don't they have it all!' If you are in the zone of desperately wanting a child and it being out of reach, almost everyone around you seems to hold what you are missing.

But what you don't see is their journey. You can't see years of fertility treatment, failed attempts at IVF, miscarriages or the tiny babies lost. If you are lucky you will have experienced none of these things; in the worst situations some couples experience them all.

But often we just don't know because we don't talk about it. Or even if we do, we then quickly sweep it under the carpet because people, myself included, get all awkward when they have to discuss sad stuff. Serious stuff. Let's just have a cup of tea and call it 'one of those things'.

Have you ever had a conversation with a friend who told you that she's miscarried and then quickly brushed it away because 'It happens all the time'? You can see that her eyes have started to water and she's struggling to make eye contact because it doesn't really matter how long she was pregnant for or how big or small the baby got – it was a life, there was so much excitement, so much potential and then suddenly it's all gone, to be treated like a common cold: grow up, get over it, everyone has them! Except a couple of paracetamol doesn't provide a quick fix when it comes to miscarriages.

Years later, when hopefully those couples have a child or children of their own, they may still feel like they are not allowed to mention their journey any more because ultimately they got their dream. But you are still allowed to feel that loss aren't you?

You see, a huge proportion of parents have been through their own personal struggles to get to where they are now - hopefully a happy place. We have.

I can't talk about the heartache of struggling to conceive as that was not our bridge to cross, although in many ways I can only imagine not having a tangible loss makes it even harder. The first time I got pregnant it was a surprise, a scary 'Can we do this?' surprise but ultimately an exciting one.

After months of horrendous all-day sickness it was finally time for our first scan. I would love to say that I was one of those mothers who looked forward to the scan but I didn't. I'm a horrible Googler of doom and I was terrified at the prospect of a missed miscarriage. So I can't tell you how relieved I was, how relieved we both were, to see a baby with a heartbeat flash up on the screen. 'Nice and strong,' the sonographer said and I relaxed back on to the bed.

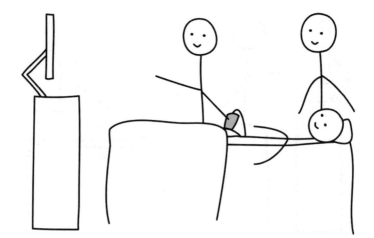

We had a heartbeat! I could see a face and hands and feet. Everything was perfect – we were one of the lucky ones.

But instead of the sonographer moving on and pointing out all of the other teeny-weeny foetus body parts, it all got a bit quiet. I didn't like it. I didn't like the shift in mood but my head was telling me it was fine because we had a heartbeat, and that's all you need isn't it?

Turns out it isn't.

Everything is a blur, another doctor comes in, more silence, no answers, we need more tests and scans. 'Things don't look hopeful for your baby,' we are told.

Out we went, glancing at the waiting room full of couples who had been us twenty minutes ago, nervous but excited. Clutching a photo of our perfect-looking imperfect baby.

There were no good news phone calls, only sad ones. The texts I'd composed in my head never got sent. I didn't get to go to the shops and buy little sleepsuits, a book of names or tiny socks. Instead a lot of waiting followed. A lot of tears, and a lot of tests. It was a horrible few weeks getting through the days, stuck in a not-knowing limbo, but ultimately we were told our baby had very little chance of survival and it was a marvel the heart was still beating at all.

I wondered how my heart kept going too.

We made a choice (if you can call it that) to say goodbye. There are people in our situation, braver than I, who may have gone ahead hoping for that miracle but I was not that strong. I don't regret the decision but there will always be an element of guilt and doubt. When I read in the papers of that one in a million baby who defied the odds it's a knife to my heart. Even now, all these years later.

Some babies are lost when nature takes its course and some parents have to make agonising decisions when faced with life-threatening diagnoses or disabilities. I have the utmost respect for the parents who step forwards, just as I do for the parents who step back, and I will always support a woman's right to choose, whatever the situation. There is no easy way out.

People deal with their grief in many different ways, I was scared by mine, I was scared it was our fate. To move forwards all I wanted was to be pregnant again and a few months later I was.

Subsequent scans with both of my pregnancies were terrifying, something to get through, to get over, each attended with pure dread. I wouldn't look at the screen until all of the checks had been done.

But we made it through two more times and were blessed with our beautiful sons. I got the family I had always wanted, and from the outside we might seem to have it all. Though there will always be a little star missing from our lives (that other people cannot see). We called her Evie and we wish she was here with us today.

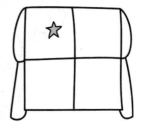

GETTING THE HUMAN OUT

Another unfortunate side-effect of being pregnant is birth. In the twenty-first century you may have thought medicine would have evolved to make birth slightly less intrusive but unfortunately not. The small person still needs to exit via your vagina, likely busting it to bits on descent.

There is also the C-section method of removal, which some people like to refer to as 'cheating', but to me major abdominal surgery doesn't sound that similar to looking over someone's shoulder in a maths test. Either way, the baby is coming out and it's not going to be pretty.

In order to attempt to give you some control over the process a lot of midwives encourage you to write a birth plan. Some people like to give this a lot of thought, and other people like to stuff their faces with cake and pretend it's not happening. Some people prioritise the impending birth and others prioritise chocolate eclairs. There is no right answer here.

After being badgered several times I finally relented and wrote two short sentences in the back of my yellow book . . .

1. Baby out safely.

2. Drugs.

I just didn't really care. I only cared about hearing that first cry and knowing it would all be OK. Everything else could be decided as we went along.

Anyway, let me tell you this, I wasn't scared of giving birth and in a strange way I was quite looking forward to it. I had always considered myself to have quite a high pain threshold so I was almost interested (I KNOW!) to see how it felt.

Lots of people had positive stories to share, although in retrospect I have a feeling not all of them were telling the truth.

So in this chapter I thought I would write a bit about how I got to be a mum for the very first time because everyone likes a good birth story don't they? Yes! (As long as it's short and to the point.)

This is how we came to meet Big Bro . . .

7 a.m.: Wake up and realise my waters have gone. Am getting mild contractions.

9 a.m.: Go to my midwife appointment. Without examining me, the midwife insists I have wet myself. I insist I have not wet myself as I know what piss looks and smells like and it is not that. 'It's wee!' she says. It's not wee. She also convinces me the baby is still very high, my contractions are Braxton Hicks and that it is too early for the baby (it is only four days before my official due date).

9.30 a.m.: Go home and tell my husband J to go to work as midwife says I am just having incontinence problems and there is nothing to worry about. J thinks midwife is a twat and stays home.

10 a.m. onwards: Spend the day eating malt loaf, timing contractions and watching TV. Contractions go on all day and get stronger and longer.

7 p.m.: Phone hospital, have a contraction down the phone at them. They tell me it doesn't sound bad enough yet and not to come in until I feel like I am dying (sort of, they may not have said dying).

8 p.m.: I self-medicate with a hot bath and paracetamol.

10 p.m.: Phone hospital and tell them I am about to die. They tell me I can come in but they will probably send me home again. We decide to risk it.

10:30 p.m.: Hospital say it's too early to be admitted to the labour ward but that I can stay. It is also too early for any drugs. Dammit.

10:45 p.m.–3 a.m.: A HORRENDOUS TIME. Feels like someone is shoving a red-hot poker up my bum and through all of my internal organs in some form of medieval torture. Everything J does or says makes me want to kill him.

3.15 a.m.: Finally someone comes to re-examine me. I am now 7cm and can go to the labour ward and have some drugs. They ask if I would like a bath. A BATH?! I WOULD NOT! I would like an epidural and I would like it now. Thank you please.

4 a.m.: Get epidural. It is the greatest thing ever invented. The sweet relief of being totally numb is the best (non) feeling in the world.

5 a.m.: We watch the sun come up over Brighton Pier, life is good.

7 a.m. onwards: Bloody hell, babies take a long time to get born! Twenty-four hours and counting and still we wait.

12 p.m.: Time to push! I still feel sod-all pain, and have been awake for nearly thirty hours, so I am practically falling asleep between contractions.

12:35 p.m.: The baby starts to get very tired too, the heart rate is dropping and it needs to come out asap. Emergency stations. Lots of people. I need an episiotomy and ventouse delivery. We are suddenly about to meet our baby. I don't know if I am ready! What if I don't love it? What if it looks funny?

12:45 p.m.: One big pull and our baby is born. No longer just an 'it' but a he! Our boy. He is here, he is beautiful. One of his eyes won't open fully, I worry something is wrong but midwife says it

just got a bit squished (to this day though, if
you look carefully, he has one eye slightly more
closed than the other).

We love him immediately, wonky eye and all.

I can't put into words an accurate description of
the relief that flooded my body at that moment. I
don't think I had let myself fully believe that I
was going to be a mum; to hold my baby safely in
my arms was something I hadn't dared to imagine.

I wish I could have bottled that feeling –
amazing, euphoric, scary and surreal all at once.
It's the reason why I'm often reluctant to say we
are 'done!' with our family, it's addictive

– despite the pain (note to self from the sensible side of your brain – you are done!).

I would love to end it there on that happy note, I couldn't wait to get back home with my new family but unfortunately we were stuck in hospital for a few days.

Breastfeeding seemed like an impossibility and I was unable to do a wee after the catheter that accompanies an epidural was removed, resulting in being re-catheterised (epidurals do have their downsides unfortunately).

I was a sorry sight. I cried because everything hurt, I cried because feeding was painful and never-ending, I cried because I hated dragging my wee bag around with me.

I cried because I hadn't slept in days. The nurses took pity on me and got me a private room, they brought me some liquid morphine (in a little shot glass!) and wheeled Big Bro out so I could finally get some rest. Soon afterwards I was a Care Bear prancing about in the clouds and sinking into my bed for the best sleep of my life.

Eventually I came back down to earth. Eventually I was able to provide the prize wee. And eventually we managed to get discharged. But before I move on to the subject of taking the baby home, I must tell you about how different Little Bro's birth was.

I decided that I needed to be more prepared this time round. I bought pain management books and worked on my breathing, which really did help – but what mostly helped was that it was a hell of a lot quicker . . .

7 a.m.: Wake up with contractions, assure J it will take ages and he goes off to work. Baby can't come right now as I am getting my roots done at the hairdresser's and THAT is the priority.

11 a.m.: Getting hair done. Making small talk with hairdresser and feeling increasingly uncomfortable. Bite lip. Don't want to cause a scene. Am British after all.

2 p.m.: Pop into Sainsbury's Local on the way home to buy malt loaf because that's what I ate first time round so – lucky?! Waters go in the cereal aisle. (When I tell people this they always ask if I got free shopping for a year as a result and I tell them no because I did what any normal person would have done and waddled the fuck out as fast as I could, hoping no one would notice. (Again – I am British!)

2:30 p.m.: Waters have meconium in them so we need to get to hospital right away. Instruct my mum to collect Big Bro from preschool and wait for J to get back from work and drive us there.

3 p.m.: While J parks car at hospital I try and take a final selfie of my fully sized bump, which I never got round to. How did this all happen so quickly?

3:15 p.m.: The contractions are coming quick so we go right to delivery. Midwife asks if a student doctor can come in to observe. I say yes, I don't care or notice who is in the room at this point.

3:30 p.m.: Getting quite uncomfortable. I have some gas and air and start punching the windowsills as per the distraction technique in pain management books.

4:20 p.m.: I need a poo!!! Apparently though it's just the baby coming down. It feels incredibly odd and heavy and not at all right.

4:30 p.m.: I need an epidural!!! Midwife asks if I can cope for twenty minutes as the baby is coming soon. I am shocked – I thought it would go on for hours. Of course I can cope for twenty minutes.

4.43 p.m.: Little Bro is born quickly and safely. It was painful but totally manageable, we are both in shock but thrilled with our second son who looks exactly like his brother.

It was different from the first time round, I wasn't lying on a bed reading magazines and falling asleep. I was an active participant, I pushed and breathed the baby out entirely of my own accord and it felt amazing (although TBH both ways have their advantages and I can confirm you get neither a medal nor a special sticker for going drug-free).

A little bit later on, when I had my legs up in stirrups and a spotlight shining on my trainwreck of a foof, I finally noticed the student doctor who was observing. He was quite fit . . .

. . . and I felt incredibly sorry for his view.

I loved being in hospital this time round, despite the fact I didn't sleep a wink all night. There was a lady in the bay next to me snoring relentlessly. The nurses had to keep waking her up when her baby cried as she didn't hear it. I couldn't understand how she could sleep so deeply. I was wide awake, partly due to the snoring, mostly due to the love bubble. I was back in the middle of it again and any reservations that I couldn't love another little person quite as much as the first were gone. It was just as amazing the second time round and I will always cherish that sleepless night we had together in hospital, when it was just us two.

Also, I personally didn't shit myself in either birth so it's not a given!

I DON'T KNOW WHAT I'M DOING

'OK you're good to go!' said the doctor. We'd
been sitting around for hours waiting for the
forms to be filled in and final checks to be done
but those words still came as a bit of a shock.
Buckling the baby into his brand new car seat
and exiting the ward felt a bit like smuggling
pick n' mix out of Woolworths up the sleeves of
my school sweater (which I obviously never did
Mum!). Was no one going to come and ask us if

we knew what the hell we were doing with this kid?

But despite feeling like total amateurs we were also incredibly excited to get home and start life as a proper little family of three. Do you remember your very first days at home with your newborn? I do.

I remember getting through the door and feeling a funny shift in the atmosphere, like everything had changed. I remember feeling so tired and so happy all at once. I remember snuggling on the sofa, greeting visitors, eating cake, admiring the flowers, passing the baby around and constantly disappearing to the bedroom to get half naked to feed him. I remember greeting midwives and crying on their shoulders, and people bringing food. I remember the precious milky smell of my son's head and the sweet buttery popcorn aroma of his filled nappy. I remember looking at all the cute clothes that people bought and laughing at the size of them.

I remember looking like absolute shit but feeling like a celebrity.

I remember the ridiculously inflated boobs, hot baths, cracked nipples and the hour I sat on the toilet carefully birthing my first poo. I remember watching crappy daytime TV and crying at the soaps, even though they weren't sad. I remember the very specific arrangement of cushions on the sofa that made it just about possible to sit down and I remember it all being made OK because I was surrounded by love.

I remember the most beautiful little boy I had ever seen feeding until he was full and then sleeping curled up in a little ball on my chest. I remember thinking it didn't seem that hard and I remember waving J back off to work feeling slightly terrified but otherwise confident I could cope looking after a baby on my own.

Then something happened. The milk coma thing stopped working. The baby was only a couple of weeks old and he had already malfunctioned.

I fed him and he remained awake, and not only that – he was unhappy awake. He was crying and he wouldn't stop. So I did what many a new mum does. I scoured the internet and devoured baby book after baby book looking for the answers.

The advice all sounded so sensible. We needed a routine and a feeding and nap schedule; instead of sleeping in our arms while we ate our lasagne one-handed, he should have a proper bedtime.

There was only one problem. He refused to get on board with the goddam book.

I was confused. All the babies in the books fed less regularly and slept much longer. Why did I get the duff version?

Not only could he not follow a simple schedule, he was also colicky in the evening and I began to dread what a lot of people term 'the witching hour' but should more accurately be described as 'the witching five hours'. I would pace about swinging him in my arms so fast I was scared he would fly across the room.

Help I thought. Help me.

'Enjoy the early days!' people said, 'it goes by so quickly!'

I remember thinking I fucking hope it does!

'It gets easier!' people said. 'You get smiles at six weeks, they stop crying as much, they start giving back.'

But I don't remember it getting easier. I remember feeling like a failure, I remember a vicious cycle of expressing milk because I was too sore to feed and then topping up with formula because I never had enough milk. I remember feeling exhausted and guilty because I'd made such a hash of it all. I remember watching breastfeeding counsellors trying to explain the perfect latch with stupid knitted boobs and willing one of them to just say 'You've done a great job but it's OK to stop now.'

I remember the reflux, the constant changes of puke-covered sleepsuits and I remember desperately trying every type of bottle and colic remedy I could get my hands on. I remember feeling lonely, even when I was surrounded by familiar faces, and I remember lying awake at night too anxious to sleep. I remember feeling utterly confused as to how and why anyone goes on to have more children. I remember looking at my son on his playmat and not knowing what to do with him, I remember feeling scared and I remember thinking what happens if I can't do this any more?

I don't know how I would have coped if I had been on my own. I used to wake in the middle of the night and have panic attacks. J was always there for me, taking over the job of the rational half of my brain that had been replaced with a fog of baby-induced paranoia. He made me book an appointment at the doctor's and I went to stay with my mum and dad.

I was lucky — with some support and packets of pills I was feeling so much better a few months later.

It's strange now when I look back on that time because despite all the stuff I remember, it also feels like I'm looking through a pane of steamed-up glass, at another version of me. I question how I ever found it so difficult to look after one small immobile baby. Having a toddler in tow who enjoys running at oncoming traffic when you are trying to breastfeed in public is surely much harder right?

But it wasn't, because this was the point in my life where everything shifted from it all being about me to it all being about somebody else. I couldn't nip to the corner shop to buy a bag of pickled onion Monster Munch, grabbing my keys and purse on my way out; I had to relearn how to live, putting another person first.

I'm not sure that anyone finds their first foray into parenting easy, even if you take to it naturally and have a chilled-out dream of a first child. The feeling is impossible to explain or prepare for, it's amazing but it's a burden; a heart that's so full of pride, love and excitement can also feel very much like one that's been broken in two.

So I can't write this with much useful advice or explanations for expectant or new parents. Nothing, no one and no words can truly prepare you for parenthood. And even if they could, your experience would be different to mine, easier (hopefully), harder (I hope not) – who knows.

However, here are a few things I have learnt along the way:

- Reading baby books and incessant Googling can help some people but for me they were the root cause of my problem. The second time round we worked out our own routine (which is kind of what you've got to do with a second baby anyway) and we were all so much happier.

This is me having a huge bonfire burning a big pile of baby books. In reality I just returned them to the library/gave them to charity shops but that doesn't sound or look quite so dramatic.

- It can be hard. It's OK to find it hard but if it feels overwhelmingly hard then you need to ask for help.
- Despite failing miserably at breastfeeding my first son I went on to successfully feed my second. I can also tell you that I notice not one iota of difference between them and the only regret I have is wasting so much time beating myself up about it.
- Some babies cry all the time because that's just what some babies do. They all stop . . . eventually.
- Despite what people tell you, you don't need to embrace every minute. Some moments, say for example when your son pukes into your actual mouth, are totally un-embraceable. Embrace what you can where you can and don't feel bad for wishing some of it away.
- You will eventually work out a system that enables you to leave the house before midday (even if it does involve a lot of swearing).
- But if you find yourself still sitting in your PJs at 6 p.m., surrounded by sicky muslins, half-eaten bowls of cereal and cups of cold tea, don't feel disheartened that you did 'nothing' all day. I'm betting your baby is clean, fed, warm and safe and that's not nothing, it's everything.

- If you are a new mum, if you know a new mum who could do with a bit of support, or even if no one ever told you twenty years ago when you needed to hear it then this is for you . . .

You are doing a brilliant job.

Just being there, and occasionally shutting yourself in the bedroom for a good scream, is still doing a brilliant job. As is hiding in the bathroom and eating a secret Twix . . . Oh and counting down the minutes until it's socially acceptable to reach for the wine is also cool (I hope).

- I didn't know what I was doing then, I still don't know what I am doing now and I'm not sure anyone else does either. Ninety-nine per cent of parenting is actually just winging it.

GET SOME NEW MATES

Many years ago before I had kids I remember staying with my friend Hannah when she had a young baby. I was just about to take a shower when she asked me to hold off because the fan in the bathroom would wake up her son. *WTF?* I thought. Why do people even have children if they are so bothered about getting them to sleep all of the time?

I was quite adamant that I wasn't going to be one of those incredibly dull people (sorry Hannah) who let their offspring overhaul their whole lives. I mean I certainly wouldn't be saying I couldn't meet for lunch at 1 p.m. because of nap time – children should fit around your plans right?

In short, I was one of those clueless pre-child idiots who need slapping about the face with a wet fish.

Kids, it turns out, are total lifejackers. Mine for example took away my ability to leave the house without three different bags, my lie-ins, the leisurely brunches and Sunday afternoons reading the paper, my youthful complexion, my desire to wear anything other than trainers, my energy, my pert boobs, the skill required to talk in proper sentences and the downtime I REALLY needed to get over hangovers. Along with, and because of, all of those things, they also started to chip away at the relationships I had with childless friends.

Protest as much as you will but a lot of the stuff you used to do just isn't going to be suitable for babies, AKA the fun police.

You see I was not 'fun, spontaneous, let's stay up all night ranking our top five crisps Katie' any more. Now most of my conversations revolved around teething, cradle cap, shit, naps (not mine obviously), sterilising and which baby slings are the best etc. Yes, to me it was interesting(ish), to me it was my whole world, but to other people a lot of it was pretty dull. Hell, at times I even reduced myself to tears over the mundanity of it all.

Do you remember those people you used to previously scorn for posting too many baby photos on Facebook? Yeh, well now that's probably you. In fact in the first few months of your baby's life it's likely you will change your Facebook photo to your baby's face, because let's face it they are much nicer, younger and cuter and you now look like shit (sorry).

So if people without kids don't want to talk to you any more because all you talk about is your kid; and if you don't want to talk to people without kids any more because all they talk about is how tired they are despite sleeping for thirteen hours last night (and then spending the morning eating bacon sandwiches in bed. Fuckers!) . . . then what do you do?

Replace them with some new ones!

One of the best ways to meet parent mates is through an antenatal class – the thought of being friends with people just because babies are about to drop out of your vaginas at approximately the same time might initially seem nauseating but worry not. You don't even have to specifically like these people, just having someone to go out for coffee with and cry at IS enough. Also for every couple sitting there asking irritating questions and finding the session empowering, there will be another thinking 'Bla bla bla what shall we have for dinner?' You choose where you best fit on that spectrum and try and sit next to the ones you like best.

Another way to meet mum mates is to do baby classes (see page 126 on reasons why you should also *not* do these classes), go to breastfeeding groups and wrap yourself around the legs of random people you see down the park. If you are a stay-at-home dad and you spot another stay-at-home dad then I imagine you just cling to him like a life raft in the middle of the Pacific Ocean during a hurricane.

Help me! If I have to discuss nipple cream one more time I might commit a murder!

Now you hopefully have some mum (or dad!) friends, let's have a think about the quality. An annoying mum friend whose baby sleeps and eats well and looks around the room smiling instead of trying to burst people's eardrums with its incessant crying is probably better than having zero mum friends (*probably* but I'm not entirely sure really), but the ideal situation is that you should try to find mum friends with a similar agenda and view to yourself.

For example, here are a few of the kinds of qualities that would attract me to another mum:

- The one with an even shitter baby than mine.
- The one who brings wine to the antenatal group picnic and is totally unapologetic about it.
- The one who evil-eyes the people giving me disapproving looks because I dared to breastfeed at a bus stop.
- The one who hands her toddler a grab bag of Wotsits so she can just breathe for five minutes.
- The one who doesn't care if I turn up with greasy hair and a suspicious-looking stain on my top.
- The one who doesn't do a sharp intake of breath because I refer to my kid as an arsehole (sometimes just like adults kids are arseholes, they just are).
- The one who generally doesn't give a rat's arse about what people think about the choices she made.
- The one who sticks her fingers down her throat and makes a fake gagging sound every time. someone brings up the topic of school catchment areas.

- The one who gives me a hug and tells me 'It's not just you.'
- The one who turns up late for Baby Sensory and swears unashamedly.

You see everyone changes when they have kids, you can't not. But it doesn't have to change the very essence of who you are. You just need to get used to surreptitiously drinking gin from a sippy cup during Rhyme Time . . . for example.

And these days when people tell me excitedly that they are expecting a child, and they say stupid shit like they will be taking their new baby to Glastonbury at four weeks old, I say one thing and think another – because apparently the other way round is considered a bit rude.

Saying VS. Thinking

Oh my gosh you are going to make such cool parents!

He he he. See you in hell.

Watching the downfall of enthusiastic parents-to-be can make a great hobby. When they 'get it' I just make sure I'm waiting with open arms and a double G&T.

Final note – don't totally get rid of your childless friends though because they are very useful for occasional blowouts. Instruct them to lead you astray so that you can totally forget you have responsibilities. And children. Everybody needs time out.

Err this really is the final note - when you emerge from the cocoon of being a parent to young children you start to emerge from the cocoon of dullness at the same time. Hannah became less dull as her kids got older, then I had kids and became the dull one, and now our kids are a little older we can go away for the weekend, get drunk and discuss what our top five favourite crisps are again. It's just the circle of life.

HOW TO GET YOUR BABY TO SLEEP THROUGH THE NIGHT

They are trying to teach me the difference between day and night but they are mistaking me for someone that gives a shit.

Some people are blessed with kids who self settle at bedtime, do twelve-hour stints and wake up at socially acceptable times like 7.30 a.m. Although it might be tempting to flick people like this hard on the forehead, bear in mind it's not really their fault. They just got lucky (or were a better person than you in a past life).

The holy grail of parenting is getting your baby to sleep through the night. For the first few months it's basically conversation currency and no one can talk or think about anything else. This is because new parents quickly learn that the love they feel for their offspring increases by approximately 500% when they are in suspended consciousness.

At first it can seem like babies are asleep all of the time. That is until you make the stupid mistake of assuming they will sleep anywhere else apart from your arms . . .

You've got to give babies some props here for being able to go from totally comatose to batshit crazy in thirty seconds.

So anyway, Baby Sleep Lesson One for me was that they slept great as long as they were on me. Sounds simple enough but err . . . How am I meant to get anything done/get any sleep myself?!

Oh I see. I'm not. Well who needs sleep anyway? (Clue: me.)

There are many things you can purchase or try to get your kids to sleep. None of them will actually work, you know this deep down in your heart, but sheer desperation will force you to buy them anyway.

I handed over thirty quid for Ewan the sodding Dream Sheep with his lulling womb noises and spent years investing in the promise of Johnson's Bedtime Baby Bath like a total numpty.

You guys made promises you couldn't keep!

SUCKERRRR!

Don't hate the players!

They tell us it's 'clinically proven' to help babies sleep better but it costs a fortune. Does it work better than the cheaper versions? And how would anyone ever know? Did they also test the babies with a cheap Aldi version and then interview them the next day?

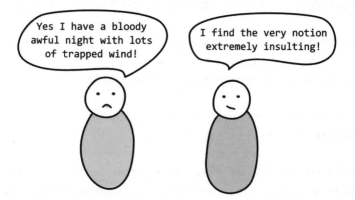

Do you feel your sleep is affected if your parents use own brand toiletries?

Yes I have a bloody awful night with lots of trapped wind!

I find the very notion extremely insulting!

When it's night-time it can often feel like your baby is awake more than they are asleep. That's because they actually are. It can also feel like your partner deserves to die for not having breasts. If you are bottle feeding and your partner is able to sleep through the baby waking up, see if he can sleep through you accidentally elbowing him in the balls. If you are doing this all on your own because you don't have a partner then massive kudos to you, I hope you have lots of gin.

When you have finished spending two hours feeding and burping your baby and laid him or her gently back down to sleep you will often find that they:

A, Vomit all over themselves
B, Shit themselves
C, Do both of the above simultaneously

Congratulations, your baby will now be up for another two hours. Yay. Go you.

This whole lack of sleep thing makes people crazy. They are desperate for the answers. A while back I overheard a conversation a mum was having with a health visitor about her six-month-old daughter. It went something like this:

Flustered mum: So I leave the room and she just starts crying, so I wait fifteen minutes before going back in but she won't stop crying - should I wait even longer?

HV: No you can't leave a baby that young to cry for fifteen minutes.

Flustered mum: But the last health visitor I saw told me to leave her for fifteen minutes. What do *you* think I should do then?

HV: Well to me it sounds like she could be overtired. Have you tried bringing her bedtime forwards?

Increasingly flustered mum: No - I was told to try putting her to bed later as perhaps she isn't tired enough . . .

HV: Well maybe it's a hunger thing, maybe you need to up her solids in the day.

Very irate and flustered mum: She's eating loads - everyone keeps telling me different stuff! How am I meant to know who is right?

Hmm, herein lies the problem - no one can tell you how to get your baby to sleep, they can only tell you what did or didn't work for them. Because get this - babies are people. Little individual people.

They do not care that Gina Ford reckons they should be sleeping through the night at eight weeks old and if they could speak they would probably be telling her to kiss their cute little bottoms.

You see as much as I like to fall asleep while watching TV in bed, you might need a screen-free room and a meditation CD. June next door likes a hot milk while reading her book and Mr Lewis three doors down knocks himself out with a large glass of red. Babies are no different – except you are not supposed to give them alcohol (which is probably the one thing that would be quite effective).

I was bloody lucky with Big Bro, he slept through the night from about four and a half months. People often asked me what the secret to my success was, and my reply? 'Er I dunno' – he just did it. In contrast Little Bro was nearly a year old before he ever slept through and is still a bloody nightmare now.

I really believe that each and every child has some sort of inbuilt sleep-through-the-night switch that flicks on at a mystery time determined at birth. And then when that time comes you will probably go and ruin it all by waking up yourself at 5 a.m. in a blind panic that they have stopped breathing.

It is unlikely that you will get back to sleep. Especially if you are breastfeeding as you have to get up and milk yourself.

The next night you will then desperately try and remember every single thing you did that day in order to replicate it and achieve the same result. A late supper, dream feed, calm bath, books, lullabies, 2.5-tog bag and long-sleeved vest . . .

Will it work? Will it fuck.

Expect to play a cat and mouse game of will or won't they for a few months because babies love to tease. And when you do (hopefully) get to the magical point of having a child who consistently sleeps through, you will likely go and ruin it by deciding to get pregnant and do it all over again.

Also, babies will turn into toddlers, and if your toddlers are anything like mine they will become masters at bedtime fuckwittery (see page 189 for more info). I'd swap 'em for a newborn any day.

'WE DON'T LIKE PEAS!'

There are not many parts of parenting that I am utterly convinced about but one thing I know for sure, I'd like my kids a whole lot better if they didn't have to eat.

It wasn't always that way of course. As a mum of an approaching six-month-old with reflux I couldn't wait to get him started on food to break the monotony of bottles, puke, bottles, bottles and more puke. By this point I wanted my steriliser to die a slow agonising death. I hope you understand.

But being a parent does funny things to your brain and my excitement soon turned to utter confusion as I realised that the simple notion of giving your baby food was actually the most complicated thing in the world. There are entire books written on the subject and I know this because I bought them (yes again, I had admittedly learnt nothing from the baby book bonfire on page 54).

The books told me I needed to make decisions and everyone around me was like 'When are you going to start?', 'How are you going to do it?', 'Will you use jars or make everything fresh?'

I was confused, I didn't really know what to do so I just started buying stuff in a blind panic to attempt to make myself look like I knew what I was doing. If in doubt – purchase. I bought an expensive steamer–blender combo thing, ice cube tray whatsits for freezing all of the batch cooking I was never going to do and a huge selection of expensive organic vegetables despite never eating organic stuff myself.

At first weaning seemed a relatively fun way to pass the time but soon it all became a bit relentless. Life seemed to revolve around a constant flow of milk and food, food and milk – it was never-ending. As soon as a bottle was finished it was snack time, as soon as snack time was finished it was time to cook dinner. FFS, babies did nothing but eat.

I realised quite early on that I was too highly strung to do pure baby-led weaning, I couldn't deal with expensive bits of mango being flung around the room (how rude!) so we did half and half.

Although I'd suggest you watch out saying that around BLW purists. I remember telling a lady at baby group, let's call her Jenny, before watching her choke on her own saliva at the existence of any such hybrid approach.

Me: For flexibility we do one meal finger food and one meal via a spoon – so half BLW and half traditional.

Jenny: BLW is for purists only. If you do any spoon-feeding at all you may not use the term BLW!

Me: OK sorry. But what if my baby wants to eat some Weetabix or cottage pie?

Jenny: In such situations you are permitted to use a spoon. You must load the spoon with food and then pass it to the baby to administer into its chosen orifice.

Me: But my baby kinda likes it in his mouth.

Jenny: Them's the rules!

Me: Who makes all the rules? The babies?

Jenny: Um . . . Spoon-feeding is the work of the devil, be gone with you!

Why Jenny actually cared is beyond me. By my reckoning, if you assist your kid getting yoghurt into his mouth as opposed to eyeball via the *EVIL* vehicle of a piece of cutlery, then the outcome is better for everyone.

But while I liked spoon-feeding certain foods I also got dead bored of pureeing. I'll admit it was relatively satisfying whipping out tubs of organic cauliflower dhal from the nappy bag but it was also pretty draining worrying about boring stuff like defrost times and reheating.

Despite my initial reservations about using jars (they were also evil right?), when I looked at the back of a jar of carrot puree it only seemed to contain carrot and no evil at all! Unless of course you believe that all carrots are intrinsically evil by nature, but I wagered not.

I make it sound like it was a long convoluted process to get to this decision but in reality it was about two days.

My weaning approach was therefore: non-mango finger foods, home-cooked meals, jars when we were out and about and sometimes a bag of Quavers because they seemed to work better than Bonjela as a teething remedy. So basically we did a bit of everything. If you've got a problem with that Jenny then fucking sue me.

Weaning the second time round was better. I just fed Little Bro whatever Big Bro was eating, which was often just what we were eating minus the salt, and that worked fine. I also didn't have to read any books.

Once we'd got over the hurdle of eating actual food and we were on full meals, there came a period where I was able to feel quite smug about my parental prowess – I had a baby who ate everything: salmon, cucumber, houmous, broccoli, couscous, cat food, sand, bits of chewing gum he found in the park. You name it, he'd eat it.

How difficult it must be to have a fussy eater I thought, although it's probably just the parents' fault for weaning them on chicken nuggets.

That was until it all went wrong and he declared that Mummy's home-made cottage pie was actually 'YUK!'. Slowly but surely as he grew, his list of acceptable foods started to diminish until, aged about two, he rejected practically everything savoury except toast, pasta and cheese. Sometimes even cheese if it wasn't cut up in the right way.

Why, why, why?! I thought. I mean what goes on in the mind of a toddler? It suddenly became clear when I went to pick him up early from preschool one day and arrived halfway through teatime.

He was always a fan of peas before, but I noticed a large pile left on his plate. 'What's wrong with the peas?' I asked. Suddenly the whole table started chanting 'Oh we don't like peas, no peas yuk, no one likes peas!'

WE DON'T LIKE PEAS!

Oh I see! There was some sort of conspiracy going on. They'd been passing memos around behind the backs of their poor unsuspecting parents . . .

A memo to all toddlers re: your diet
I've noticed an alarming trend at preschool, some of my fellows seem to be eating what is presented to them on their plates without query. I have also witnessed some voluntary consumption of vegetables. It makes me sick.

Take heed people, follow these simple rules and exert some fricking authority!

- *Set the tone – spend a week detoxing on jam toast.*
- *Refuse anything but Cheerios for breakfast. Have them without milk on Mondays, Thursdays and every other Friday. Hyperventilate if they get this wrong.*
- *Don't try anything new EVER.*
- *Just because you liked something yesterday does not mean you have to like it again today. It is perfectly acceptable to change your mind and you do not have to explain yourself.*
- *Fruit as a pudding is bullshit.*
- *Be suspicious of anything that was recently alive. Beige, dead-looking stuff is safer.*
- *Request a wide variety of food at the supermarket and then a) deny all knowledge of it upon your return home or b) allow it to be cooked first and then say you don't like it.*
- *Spend some time revising brand names so that you can legitimately refuse cheaper derivatives.*

- *Any amount of cooking or food preparation time above thirty seconds is wholly unacceptable.*
- *Ask for updates of when things will be ready every ten seconds, protest with your fists on the floor if things are taking too long. This may result in the meal being served half frozen but it doesn't matter as you are not going to eat it anyway.*
- *No eating on Wednesday afternoons, just cos.*
- *Make sure you have a spoon, knife and two forks with all meals and then eat with your hands.*
- *Only ever use one specific plate. Flip out if it is dirty.*
- *Deposit as much of your meal off the side of the table as possible. They say they 'spend their whole life cleaning the kitchen floor', help make it a reality.*
- *Don't eat that sweetcorn stuff. It sounds nicer than other vegetables but it's just yellow peas.*
- *Kick people who describe broccoli as 'little trees' in the shins. It's condescending and it's disgusting.*
- *Avocado – WTF? – NO.*
- *Avoid anything with sauce as there is a risk it contains blended veg.*
- *Never drink water. They say 'You will drink it when you're thirsty', don't. Get admitted to hospital with dehydration. That'll learn 'em.*
- *Always say you are hungry when you are in the bath.*

- *Train your body clock to wake up for midnight bananas.*
- *Casseroles, stews and pies are not to be trusted.*
- *Weetabix are derogatory.*
- *Sweet potato chips are insulting.*
- *Food that is arranged into faces or stupid sodding farm animals should be hurled across the room in fury.*

AHA! Suddenly it all became clear and it was as I'd always suspected. Toddlers are far smarter than they let you believe and they are plotting our downfall.

So if you have a fussy eater (I have two now, lucky me) then there are a couple of things you can do:

1. Cook things they like, and if that means two different meals for the family then so be it.

2. Hold firm with a like it or lump it approach. I mean they won't starve will they?

I've tried number 2 and honestly believe it depends on your kids. At three years old, the peak of fussy eating in my experience, Little Bro will go all day on thin air. He's skinny and stubborn and I might be weak but I can't let him go to bed hungry (the selfish reason is that it also means he won't wake at 4 a.m. demanding Coco Pops).

So I ditched all of my lofty ideals (which seems to be my parenting thing anyway) and reasoned that we are alive, we are happy, and if something relatively healthy goes into their tummies once or twice a day then that's going down as a win.

Psssst ... sometimes I still do stuff like squirt canned cream directly into their gobs, because what it does to their faces - you just can't bottle it.

Stuff you should probably stop
doing if you have fussy eaters...
(that I will never stop doing)

Life's for living eh?

THE MILESTONES THAT MATTER

Today I projectile shat over mummy's cashmere jumper!

Now to be honest, Mummy is a fucking idiot for wearing cashmere around a baby full stop. People who do that deserve to get shat on. I don't own cashmere anything because I can't have nice things, but I certainly remember the day Big Bro did a poo that shot two metres across the lounge and hit my Primark slippers.

In contrast I can't remember the exact day either of my sons smiled for the first time, but I do remember the weeks of analysis over whether it was wind or not and I do remember getting a bit bored talking about it.

As for rolling over, what bit of difference does that even make? It just means babies get stuck with their faces up against a plug socket and where's the benefit in that?

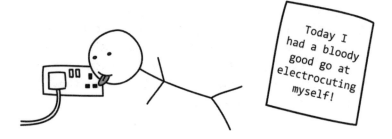

But you are always going to get parents who get obsessed with hitting milestones 'on time' or - even better - earlier. It's almost as if people spend more time worrying about milestones than they do actually trying to teach their kids the required skills to achieve them.

A random mum: I'm panicking, I'm panicking! He should be clapping by now!

A person who talks sense: Don't worry, all babies do things at their own pace.

A random mum: But people are going to think he's stupid!

A person who talks sense: Well what does he do when you show him how to clap?

A random mum: I don't know because I spend all day on BabyCentre freaking out. Surely they just learn it from CBeebies anyway? They never seem to stop bloody clapping on that.

A person who talks sense: True.

What I don't get is why people are so concerned with all the boring, run-of-the-mill milestones anyway. Yes clapping's nice but I'd much rather have a timeline of events detailing when they might start to fuck me over.

To be honest I couldn't give a rat's arse when my son masters the pincer grip, how about someone tells me when he will start nicking money out of my handbag?

Today I
ate a
tenner!

I know roughly when I might expect to hear the word 'Mama' but why do none of the books tell me the average age you might expect to get sworn at in public?

Today I shouted 'BOLLOCKS' in the frozen aisle

Who cares when they start sitting? What I want to know is when they start hitting!

Today I made Mummy cry three times!

At six months they might cut their first tooth but when will they bite hard enough to draw blood?

Stacking cups is all well and good but at what age might you expect them to start redecorating your home with obscene graffiti?

Whoop dee doo they can grasp a toy!

WHEN ARE THEY GOING TO BE ABLE TO GRASP REALITY?!?!?

I want conversations like this to be more socially acceptable . . .

Other mum: Our sons look similar ages, how old is yours?

Me: Sixteen months.

Other mum: Such a great age isn't it?

Me: SO great.

Other mum: He's started putting three words together now, it's pretty amazing.

Me: Yep pretty amazing. Can he drag a stool over to your front door, unlatch it and let himself out?

Other mum: Um, no . . .

Me: Hmm sounds like a bit of an idiot then.

Am I joking? I bloody well wish I was. Sixteen months. Sixteen!

So the only advice I have to offer on the subject is that if, by two years old, your kid has not smashed your smartphone by throwing it across the room in a furious rage about something completely insignificant, then maybe it's worth getting them assessed for developmental delay.

ONE FOR THE DADS

So we've talked quite a lot about being a mum huh? It's inevitable - I am one so I can only talk on behalf of myself. But parenthood is not just for mums, so I thought we'd best give a little nod to the dads too.

Although if you're expecting a chapter about how useless they are then I'm sorry but you won't find it here. Sure dads do a lot of stupid stuff – J on more than one occasion has strapped the kids into the car, and only on arriving at the destination discovered that they do not have any shoes on (cue emergency footwear purchases and lots of colourful language), but it's not because he's a useless dad, it's just because he's generally a bit stupid sometimes. But then so am I, there are plenty of examples of that in this here book.

And sure there are the crap dads, the lazy dads, the dads who never seem to be there and the dads who leave (equally applicable to mums), but let's for a minute talk about the dads who take their role seriously . . .

You see, things are changing, men are no longer expected to stay out of the delivery room, go straight to the pub to wet the baby's head and not change a single nappy. Nowadays splitting the responsibility equally is becoming the norm. Why shouldn't dads be able to put their kids to bed? To pack up the changing bag and look after them on their own for a weekend? Surely they should be able to feed, clothe and occupy their own children without a detailed set of instructions (at least eventually)? Not just because it's good for the mums (it is), or even that it's good for the dads (it totally is) but also because it's good for their children; the best lesson they'll ever get on equality starts right there.

It's not 'sweet' to see a dad take his children to the sodding park on his own, it's just called 'normal'. It is not 'lucky' to have a husband who gets up to his kids in the night, it's just called 'parenting'. It's not 'admirable' to see a man feeding his own baby, it's just called 'not being a total dick'.

So bearing all of that in mind I thought I'd ask J to share a few of his own thoughts, worries and high points of being a dad because how can I write a book about parenthood without asking the one who's standing by my side and sharing the job with me (in all honesty he freaked out about doing this because he was adamant he couldn't write and he also asked me to put a warning up front saying THIS IS NOT GOING TO BE FUNNY, although TBH I think he's done rather well. He didn't do the drawings though, I obviously spent years in fine art school to get my stick man technique right *cough cough*).

Anyway, here we go . . .

Are we ready?
Can we afford this?
How will we manage?
Will he like Star Wars?
What football team will
he support?
Shall we have another?
Can we get a dog?

If you'd asked me to describe my first night of being a dad I'd say 'strange'. You've been awake for hours, been through phases of panic, dreamlike calm and immense worry and the next thing you know you're sent home. Alone. Leaving the two most important people in your life in hospital. It was a night like no other; a normal night at home for me would mean relaxing with a film, music or playing Xbox, but this night was just spent sitting, in awe of what just happened, and wishing the time away to get back and see them.

I had two weeks off for paternity leave before having to go back to work. The first few days were all about settling into family life, watching our brand new boy shit, eat and sleep, and also enjoying it. The good thing about babies is that they sleep. A lot. Well ours did anyway, at least at first. They also don't do much, so as it was summer and we'd just moved to a new area we were able to get out and about loads (and by that I mean visit pub gardens).

The worst bit about the first few weeks was some of the unknowns. We worried so much about little things: was he sleeping properly? Was he taking enough milk? Was he putting on enough weight? etc. It became clear that breastfeeding wasn't going to be an option for Katie and she became quite ill. There's a lot of pressure put on mothers to breastfeed, and in some cases it just isn't possible. I tried to reassure her as much as I could that it really didn't matter but it's one of those areas where as a dad you can end up feeling quite powerless to help.

And then before I knew it, it was back to work and the four-hour daily commute to London. One of my clients joked 'Come back to work when you need a rest!' and he was right, although in a different way. Looking after the baby and Katie was physically tough, getting used to less sleep in the first few months was difficult, I was keeping myself awake listening to irregular breathing (apparently totally normal) and then I was in and out of bed for feeds, milk prep and sterilising. The second time round she was able to breastfeed just fine, which was weird because I felt like I wasn't as useful, particularly for night feeds. I felt pretty guilty as often I'd just sleep through it all.

I never wanted to be a weekend dad though, I always wanted to be as involved as I could in their lives from the off. I know a lot of the responsibility can fall to the mum in the early days because they are often the ones doing the majority of the care but I wanted to be able to do anything Katie could (within reason) if nothing else so she could have a bit of a break. I think sometimes people think dads have it easy as they're often the ones out working but I felt like I was missing out on a lot too. Seeing photos and watching videos isn't the same as actually being there.

And work isn't often much of a break, the commute can be a nightmare, lunch is eaten at my desk or doesn't happen and often I just feel like I'm firefighting all day – so I have felt some resentment when I've heard about Katie's day in comparison but I know in reality that going for coffee with friends isn't as idyllic as it sounds. I guess the grass always seems greener and you can each forget the challenges the other faces when you're not doing that job day in and day out.

Going out for coffee

Imagined   Actual

I sometimes have to travel for work. Not that often, but it can be a couple of times a month. The boys are always sad when I tell them I'm going to be away for even a night so my time with them is very precious: the TV wind-down on the sofa after work, reading stories before bed, brushing mud off their hands after falling over in the woods, the big cuddles when they get tired/angry/upset. Our weekends are our family *time so we tend to do stuff as a four, but we also try to give each other a little time out . . . Katie's easily pleased reading a good book in the bath.*

Being the only one working (for the first year) put some pressure on me. I place a lot of value on security and that's even more of a concern when my salary was the only thing paying the mortgage and keeping the cupboards stocked. I was juggling work as well as trying to be an active dad and it became clear that the daily commute wasn't working. I wasn't seeing my new boy as much as I wanted to, so when an opportunity came up to work closer to home I snapped it up. It felt like a risk at the time and it meant a salary cut but the quality of life for us as a family more than made up for it.

There is so much I enjoy about parenthood. Taking Big Bro out on his bike for the first time was a real highlight. He just got it. Seriously, it took about twenty seconds and he was off. No one can prepare you for that rush of pride you get seeing your child do something for the first time. Although cue crippling fear every time he rides along a pavement and a car comes near. No one can prepare you for the heart palpitations either.

Then there's the hard parts, the stuff I struggle with. I get frustrated that I don't have a lot of time for my hobbies any more, I love photography, music and gaming but now it's a case of fitting in what I can when I can. I lack patience around the boys sometimes too and I don't like having to raise my voice at them. But then there's those quiet moments, you're building Lego, making cars out of Play-Doh, colouring, reading, watching TV and they just stop, look up and say . . .

Big Bro: *Daddy?*
Me: *Yes mate?*
Big Bro: *I love you.*

And everything is just fine. All the tantrums, squabbles, annoyingly repetitive 'why?' conversations, the refusals to eat, get dressed, go to sleep, they're all gone.

And it can't have been that bad can it? Because we did have another! I think sometimes people think there are negatives to having two of the same sex but it's great because they are so similar. At first we had a lot of issues with jealousy but now they are starting to play together more and more. Of course they squabble over stuff and hit each other with makeshift weapons too but behind all the bravado you can see they care about each other. I hope they'll always be good friends.

They're changing a lot these days, as is my relationship with them. I help Big Bro out when he gets stuck on Sonic the Hedgehog and kick a ball about with Little Bro. We are starting to do stuff together that I get a lot out of too - they LOVE Star Wars (thank fuck) and I'm praying they'll be Arsenal fans too.

Most of all my job as a dad is to be the best support I can for my family. They all need different things and I'm supposed to know, whether that's finding toy cars under the fridge, working out why they don't want to go to school, giving cuddles, telling them off or mixing a good G&T when we finally get them into bed. I hope I'm doing OK.

He's not perfect, who is? But he's a good dad. I might even change that to 'great' if he would stop forgetting their bloody shoes, so yeh . . . I think he's doing OK.

P.S. I know there will be single mums reading this, maybe even some single dads and maybe some parents, who are shouldering the responsibility completely alone. Hats off, bow down. I hope you realise how awesome you are!

THE CHANGE

Toddler Psychology Explained...

Things I liked this morning

Things I like this afternoon

Flowers

Sunshine

Cheese on toast

Other people

I remember a big change in both my boys when they turned one. What an age! Suddenly they were doing adult things like walking and talking; it was amazing to see them start to develop their own little personalities and quirks.

How can you not find joy in a toddler's confidence, zest and vigour for life? Wouldn't it be amazing

if we could all carry just a dash of that magic
into adulthood?

They see something they like and they take it,
they see somebody else doing something they don't
like and they whack them out of the way. They are
always running and exploring, always wanting to
know what's on the other side of the door. They
find pure wonder in a manky cigarette butt and they
laugh with the whole of their bodies at something
that, quite frankly, isn't even that funny. They
stomp through the world like they own the whole
fricking thing.

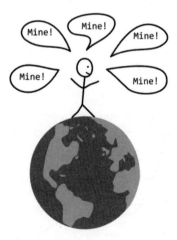

Toddlers, wow, they are (briefly) so amazing to parent. You spend so much time saying 'Did you just see that? Did you hear what he just said!' They can do practically nothing that isn't dead cute.

But all good things come to an end.

I remember lying on the sofa minding my own business (yes, yes my mistake), when Little Bro wandered up and punched me in the face with his Tommee Tippee cup. The blow was hard, for a not quite two-year-old, and as I watched the bruise rise around my left eye I couldn't help but think it was somewhat metaphorical – signifying that the baby days were well and truly over.

Welcome to the TERRIBLE TWOS (which actually in my experience starts somewhere around fourteen months and goes on until . . . well even at six Big Bro is not totally over it), basically characterised by small humans getting extremely pissed off by completely random, and quite frankly often bizarre, things.

Apologies but your dear sweet bumbling child will become possessed by an inner demon for the foreseeable future, their once pliable little body working against your every move.

No longer bendy in the middle

Uncooperative limbs

I'm not going to lie, it can be bloody scary. I recall Big Bro tantrumming to the extent that his face turned deep blue and his body lay jerking on the floor. I remember screaming, convinced that he was having some sort of seizure and dashing for my phone to call 999. As it turned out he was just a 'bit' pissed off that I had broken his banana in half and at that moment all the anger at being given an incomplete bit of fruit was deemed more significant than actually - just breathing.

BBR
(Broken Banana Rage)

Oh I see.

And of course it didn't stop there. Here are just a few of the things that I have found to really piss a toddler off:

- Being buckled into the buggy without a biscuit
- Seeing a bus or train and not being on it
- Not being allowed to tip your water all over yourself
- Being wet because you tipped your water all over yourself
- A finite supply of blueberries
- Not being able to feed the cat yoghurt
- The cat not liking yoghurt
- Not being able to draw on the table
- Not being able to draw
- Not being able to eat pens
- Not being able to eat Play-Doh
- Eating Play-Doh
- Eating soil
- Eating soap
- Being hungry because you won't eat any actual food
- Not being allowed to store pen lids in your mouth
- Wanting to bend non-bendy things
- Breaking things by bending them
- The general laws of physics
- Not being allowed to throw objects of your choosing out of windows
- Someone else touching your scooter
- Someone else looking at your scooter
- Wet feet after purposely jumping in puddles
- Bean juice on your hands after eating beans with your hands

- Not being allowed to bash the TV with a sword
- Your socks being on slightly twisted
- Not being able to take your socks off by yourself
- Not having socks on
- Socks
- Wearing gloves
- Having cold hands
- Sliced, as opposed to cubed, cheese
- Pigeons

And of course that list is by no means exhaustive. I could go on . . . and on . . . and on . . . but even then it wouldn't be much use because what pisses off a toddler in one particular moment could then go on to be their very favourite thing the next. Take train sets for example, are they a much-loved toy or will the tracks find better use as a murder weapon?

Toddlers are properly bonkers I tell you. We could be happily getting ready for a trip to the park and just as we are about to leave Little Bro will decide that he will only go if he is naked. He will run head-first into a table and then expect me to take the blame. He will decide to get seriously insulted by the colour of the cup (THAT HE BLOODY CHOSE THAT MORNING) when we are tirelessly wandering around the IKEA self-serve looking for the last component of a very complicated Pax wardrobe configuration.

It wouldn't be half as bad if it were all directed at me but much is inflicted on the general public. Give us a packed-out train carriage or elevator and he'll be rubbing his hands together in glee before taking an angry protest shit. This is why we won't be going on the London Eye any time soon.

And it's incessant is it not? I'll respond with a nervous giggle to his request for 'blue cat ice-cream' (?!) but he'll get louder and louder and louder and go on and on and on until he's forgotten what he even wanted, I had no clue in the first place and before long we are both crying proper tears as people look on in disgust.

Anyway, so now we've established that small children can be a total pain in the arse, I bet you are wondering what the best way to deal with them is? I'd suggest booking them into nursery for a few extra hours so you can spend some time alone in a dark room. Anything other than that then I'm sorry you'll have to buy a different book.

There is some relief in knowing that this is just a phase. Just like everything else in parenting is a phase, a long, never-seemingly-having-an-end-in-sight phase that is followed by what people take delight in telling you - an even worse phase.

Yes it can be hard to remember your child's good points when they are sprawled out beneath your feet, pounding the floor with their fists because you won't let them cook Playmobil people in the microwave, but please know that it won't last for ever. One day they will, finally, appreciate all you have done for them.

One day they will bound up to you all bright, breezy and full of smiles and inform you: 'Mummy, I am cuts you into pieces so I can build a house out of you' while hacking at your leg with a plastic saw.

Parenthood - *'Because I'm worth it'*.

FILLING UP THE DAY

When I get woken up at whatever godforsaken time my children decide is morning, the first thing on my mind is coffee, lots of lovely coffee, and then WTF are we going to do all day? The answer is – activities! In this chapter I have compiled a list of my top 'fun' things to do with small children, cleverly designed to help fill up the day until you get to the bedtime hour*.

*Gin time. I meant gin time.

Baby classes

Baby classes are great. So many to choose from – Sing and Sign, Baby Sensory, Rhyme Time, Little Poppets Pilates, Bilingual Babes, Tiny Toys Advanced Maths, Criminal Law for Cheeky Cherubs . . . I may have made a couple of them up but you get my drift.

Usually you will need to fork out a whacking great sum of money up front despite only being able to attend about half the sessions, but that's OK because paying £20 per class to feel like an inadequate mother standing in the corner of a room with a screaming infant is great value!

This is a picture of me (pictured on the left) at a baby massage class to help demonstrate that point. TBH I don't think anyone was having much fun apart from the lady at the front with a pocket full of cash and without a greasy pissed-off baby.

Many of the classes are also billed as being intellectually stimulating for your child but in actual fact they provide less stimulation than an empty bag of crisps.

It's worth bearing in mind that packets of crisps cost a fraction of the price of Mummy and Me Yoga and they can be purchased in most pubs. Just saying.

TOP TIP – this is from my friends Charlie and Matt. Teach your kids that a pub is actually called a 'café'. 'Mummy took me to the café at the weekend' sounds like a much more wholesome activity. One of our local pubs has got a great outside play area and we call that one 'the park'.

Playgroup

When your baby and you get fed up with baby classes you can move on to playgroups. These cost a quid or two and for that you get perimeters, mess that is not yours to clean up, a cup of crap coffee and a custard cream!

Another name I like to call playgroup is BSA (Biscuit Stalkers Anonymous) because most of the kids there have a dependence on pink wafer biscuits akin to a methamphetamine addiction.

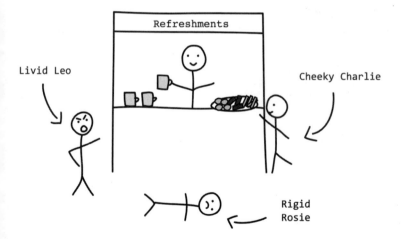

On the whole I like playgroups; some people avoid them as they don't like having to discuss the weather with strangers but I'd rather converse with another actual person than the oven so we do go. However, they are certainly not without fault.

The main issue I have with playgroups is that there is always one specific toy that every child wants, usually a ride-on. My heart sinks every time I walk through the doors and see a lone Cozy Coupe with a fan base of thirty.

I can't be the only parent out there who has dreamt about breaking into playgroup at night and sacrificing THAT TOY in some sort of ritual to the gods of parental sanity.

Then there are the days you end up at a group with ridiculously jolly staff who have the concept of playgroup all back to front . . .

This is NOT what playgroup is about. Playgroup is about feral kids foraging for bits of squished-up raisins on the bottoms of each other's shoes while the parents bitch about what a rubbish night's sleep they had and/or hide in the corner looking up pictures of other people's holidays on their phone. Everyone's happy (sort of).

Another popular thing to do at playgroup is biting. The parallels between playgroup and an episode of *The Walking Dead* are pretty uncanny if you stop and think about it.

After what feels like eternity someone will announce 'TIDY UP TIME', which means you've just got to get through the singing and then you can go back home and stick the telly on for a bit.

Everyone looks a bit glazed over by this point . . .

Oh dear, the lady on the end seems to be crying, I think her name is Rachel.

Are you OK Rachel?

Rachel is not OK. Rachel is literally bored to tears. Rachel wonders if she will be taking her daughter to playgroup FORFUCKINGEVER!

Don't worry Rachel she'll be a teenager before you know it, and then you can enjoy quality time staring at your phone at 3 a.m. praying that she doesn't get pregnant.

Soft play

We have a few soft play options near us; the nicer posher ones that cost about £50 to get in and the one round the corner, which is a bit old, a bit dirty and a bit violent. I usually go with the latter, cos that's just how we roll.

Your enjoyment of soft play will largely be determined by which parental category you fit into:

Category 1 – The parents of older kids who get to sit down, read *Grazia*, drink steaming hot coffee and deserve to die.

I'm not going to lie. I wish I was in this category, dicking about on Facebook and occasionally shouting half-arsed apologies on behalf of my ill-behaved child.

Why does soft play make children so brutal? Also why is it even called soft play when it's bloody hardcore?!

Anyway let's get on to the second category. *Sobs a bit* MY group . . .

Category 2 – The parents of younger kids who follow their toddlers around while trying to ensure the older kids (whose parents are too busy reading *Grazia*) don't take their little ones out with a drop kick to the head.

Big Bro is no problem, he runs off and comes back every fifteen minutes or so to shout his snack demands at me; but Little Bro is so disappointingly irresponsible.

Just a little tip here – eat three Snickers before you leave the house and take some of those energy gel pack things that marathon runners use because BLOODY HELL . . .

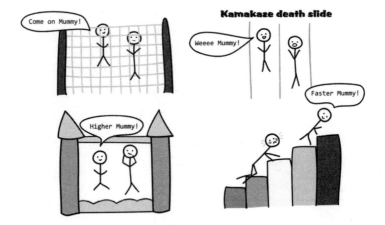

I think I died for a bit on rainbow Mount Vesuvius there. Thank God for the kid who brought me back to life by dribbling a mouthful of Capri-Sun on my face.

IT SAYS NO FOOD OR DRINK ON THE PLAY EQUIPMENT YOU LITTLE TWAT!

And of course the category 1s are ready and waiting to shoot you patronising, sympathetic glances as you try and exit the life-size lucky dip that is the ball pool, with some semblance of dignity (I won a half-eaten KitKat and a snotty wet wipe in there once. It was a special day). Don't worry though smug parents! I have made a mental note to do exactly the same when Little Bro is big enough to defend himself and you accidentally get pregnant at forty and revert back to a category 2 ☺

The park

When children say they want to go to the park it can fill a parent's heart with pure dread. Mostly because it doesn't matter how long you stay – three hours, four hours, five! – kids always feel like they've been short-changed.

Depiction A:
Going to the park

Depiction B:
The journey home

On particularly bad, mind-numbingly dull days we might even go to the park twice. Sometimes we see other parents who have been there twice and sometimes we can have the exact same conversations twice. Sometimes it can feel a little bit like *Groundhog Day*. Because it basically is.

In our local park we used to have four baby swings in the toddler area, but after a recent playground refurbishment, there are now only two baby swings. Toddlers lay flailing on the floor unable to understand why they would have to wait so long for their swing fix. There was a public outcry, everyone was up in arms.

But the most depressing thing of all is that I have now had the above conversation about 237 times in the past six months. I try, I try as hard as I can to shut up but I cannot stop the words from tumbling out of my mouth. It's like now I'm a parent small talk is my autopilot.

stabs self in eye with own finger

If you really don't like small talk perhaps try passing the time by stalking your inappropriate celebrity crushes on Instagram. Just make sure you do it behind a tree to avoid judgemental glances from people who are better at parenting than you.

Home-based play

It's lovely to occasionally spend a day trapped inside with no chance of escape. It might be raining or you might not be able to find the will to put proper clothing on etc.

Immobile babies are relatively easy to entertain at home. Just shove them in the Jumperoo (God I miss that massive ugly hulk of plastic) and then you can watch *MasterChef* on catch-up.

For older children you could destroy your house by baking a cake or partaking in some crafting.

If you fancy feeling massively shit about yourself for a few days then why not look for some inspiration on Pinterest? The last time I let my eyes look at that site I then had to go spend an hour rocking backwards and forwards in a corner. Also kids ALWAYS spoil crafting for me.

Another thing mine have always enjoyed doing is pushing cars around on the floor and making brmmm brmmm sounds, which is, how to put this nicely . . .

REALLY FUCKING BORING.

Perhaps you might like to get carpet burns on your knees by pretending to be a friendly ride-giving tiger instead?

NO.

Technology

Let's end with one of my favourites, which is technology-based LEARNING. CBeebies IS educational, so there, and I don't know about you but my kids' faces look particularly beautiful lit up by the soft glow of an iPad.

Yes we may have managed to bring up kids just fine before tablets and smartphones came into existence, but we managed just fine before ceramic hair-straighteners too (actually I'm wrong – we had frizzy hair and terrible fringes).

Haters gonna hate but sometimes using the tech is necessary so you can get stuff done around the house. And you only need to visit your local pub on a Sunday lunchtime and do a quick tally of the parents necking bottles of Pinot Noir while their kids are hooked up to the 'digital babysitter' to see that it's just how middle-class people parent these days.

The key word here is balance.

It's certainly time to cut back when your kids start talking in American accents and think another name for human beings is 'YouTubers'.

SHIT.

(Although the above sketch is not entirely accurate as mine would never voluntarily put something in the bin.)

My point is that if you are frequently doing all of the aforementioned activities then you really don't need to feel bad about doing a little of this last one. If your kids are anything like mine then they will self-police their tablet time anyway – more often than not preferring to poke me up the bum with a lightsaber.

If you are still struggling with your concern then please feel free to go and say a little prayer for them. I'd do it myself but I'm too busy worrying about real-world stuff like climate change and whether Jesse from *Breaking Bad* eventually managed to turn his life around.

GOODBYE SWEET NAPS

Roses are red,
Violets are blue,
I've decided I shan't be napping ever again,
So screw you!

I liked it when my kids took naps (yep 'liked' as in past tense), they were a great way to have a bit of time off to do nice things for myself . . . such as emptying the dishwasher or putting some laundry away.

When Big Bro dropped all daytime sleeps before his second birthday I assumed that such a gross injustice could only be explained as a blip in the great scheme of fair nap distribution. When Little Bro did the exact same thing I realised there was no such scheme.

I just don't get it! Why the hell would they want to turn down a lovely, relaxing, revitalising, cosy, comfy (OK I'll shut up now) nap? If only you could ask them . . .

Me: So um, I was wondering . . . why don't you want to nap any more?

Little Bro: Things to do, people to see. You know how it is when you're twenty-one months old. The world is so fresh and EXCITING!

Me: Most other kids your age nap you know . . .

Little Bro: Most other kids my age are pansies.

Me: Napping is not a sign of weakness, a nice post-lunch snooze is very normal.

Little Bro: Fuck normal.

Me: The baby books suggest most kids—

Little Bro: Fuck the baby books.

Me: —continue napping until around three!

Little Bro: What don't you get here? NAPS ARE FOR CHUMPS!

Me: You'd feel a lot better if you napped you know . . .

Little Bro: You'd feel a lot better if you stopped being so bloody anal about napping!

Me: I wish I could have a nap.

Little Bro: Here we go again . . . 'Woe is me, boo hoo hoo, FML.' If you don't stop banging on I'll change my wake-up time to 4 a.m.

Me: OK OK let's not do anything drastic! It's just I really think that, at your age—

Little Bro: Oh cut the crap. We both know who you are thinking about here. Who benefits most from my naps huh? HUH??

Me: I don't know what you mean?

Little Bro: I see you nervously clutching *Stylist* magazine and eyeing the Sky box. You look like you need a wee too . . . waiting until I go to sleep so you can do it on your own perchance?

Me: That's just ridiculous. You make it sound like going to the loo on my own would be a luxury!

Little Bro: Would it?

Me: Well yes but . . .

Little Bro: Come on, what've you got loaded up on that thing? Last night's *Made in Chelsea*? *The Apprentice*? Hoping to drink a nice cup of coffee without having to microwave it three times are we?

Me: I'm only ever thinking about you!

Little Bro: Right, I'm not napping OK so don't bother. If you put me in my cot I'll just go fucking mental and throw myself over the side. And you don't want to be having to explain yourself down A&E again do you?

Me: No.

Little Bro: Good. So let's make this EVEN clearer for you. I nap at nursery, I eat at nursery. I don't nap at home and I don't eat at home! Got it?

Me: Well sort of but, um, just wondering if you would consider swapping that around so you do the cooperative things at home?

Little Bro: What do you think?

Me: No?

Little Bro: Good. Sorted. OK park time – let's do this!

Me: But it's raining.

Little Bro: I SAID IT'S PARK TIME!!!!!!!!!!!!!!!

Me: People look at me weirdly when we are the only ones stupid enough to go to the park in the rain . . .

Little Bro: Mac. On. Now.

Me: FFS.

Oh and if you read this chapter hoping to get some tips on how to get your kid napping again then you are looking firmly in the wrong place. It's over.* In my opinion there is nothing more soul-destroying than trying to convince somebody to sleep when you would like nothing more than a quick twenty winks yourself. Ain't nobody got no time for that.

*Apart from inappropriate naps at 5.45 p.m. or in the car three minutes before you arrive at your destination.

I WANT IT ALL
(BUT I'M MESSING EVERYTHING UP)

One of the biggest decisions you have to make as a mum is figuring out what to do when maternity leave finishes and you are due to return to work. There are so many factors to consider – is it financially viable? What about childcare? Is your employer flexible? What happens if your kids get sick? Will your boss be understanding if a cup of apple juice gets accidentally-on-purpose spilt over your new work laptop? Is it OK to show up at the office with Cheerios in your hair? Are you still capable of 'blue-sky thinking', 'getting your ducks in a row', 'picking the low-hanging fruit' and 'developing a holistic approach'? More importantly – do you even care?

There is no doubt about it, having children makes working more difficult. But can you be the mum you want to be and have a career to boot? Is it really possible to have it all?

I think emotions run high on this topic so it's one of the trickiest subjects to discuss. Every single mum faces her own challenges based on her working status . . .

The stay-at-home mum

Let's first talk about the mum who chooses to stay at home with her children. Maybe she has given up a career to prioritise raising them or maybe that was always her focus in the first place. This mum is doing exactly what she wants so she has it easy right? No. The problem is when other people think she is lazy, unmotivated or setting a bad example to her children about work ethic. When people ask her what she does she might meekly reply 'Oh I'm just a mum.' There is no such thing as 'just' a mum. This lady is selfless and awesome, ask her 'what she does all day' at your peril.

The reluctant stay-at-home mum

I feel frustrated for this mum. She's motivated and experienced and has a lot to offer but the roles she would like to apply for are not flexible, don't fit around raising children or they don't pay enough money to cover the cost of childcare. She's grateful for the time she has with her kids but feels let down by a society that is still not focused enough on supporting her return to work.

The full-time working mum

This mum's career is important to her. She may sometimes feel guilty about missing out on her children's younger days but she also realises that being a full-time parent is not for her. We don't need to feel sorry for her children (they are well looked after) and we don't need to ask 'Why did you even have kids in the first place?'

(she loves them fiercely). Ultimately she knows that in order for her children to be happy she needs to be happy too and this is what works for her family.

The reluctant working mum

I really feel for this mum, she doesn't want to work as much as she does but it's the only option for her family – they simply can't afford for her not to. She'd rather be at home or doing fewer hours, so she needs to be made to feel bad about her 'choices' like she needs a hole in the fricking head. If this is you please cut yourself some slack (and buy yourself a big bottle of gin).

The part-time working mum

This woman has the best of both worlds right? The perfect balance between career and parenthood. Unfortunately though, part-time work doesn't always mean part-time and this woman often struggles to get everything done during her working hours. Consequently she feels she is letting both her employer and family down. Despite being highly qualified she might feel overly grateful towards her employer for their flexibility (which is bollocks) and she might also feel undeserving of pay rises or promotions over her full-time colleagues (which is also bollocks).

The self-employed mum

The self-employed mum sees many advantages. She works for herself and can choose her own hours; she can take the kids to school and attend their class assemblies. But the problem for the self-employed mum is that because she CAN always be there she feels very guilty when she isn't. She organises her work to fit in around the children and makes up her hours in the evening before crawling into bed at midnight and stressing about her unreliable income. Self-employed mum, like most of the above mums, is fucking knackered.

The full-time working dad

Judgements – none. Oh to be a dad!

The stay-at-home dad

Apart from this one, who I imagine gets a lot of flak for being a total ninny-knickers when what he actually deserves is a bloody accolade for realising that his career is not automatically more important than his partner's just because he has a penis.

So the question is, who has it the easiest?

I've been a stay-at-home mum, I've been a part-time working mum and I am now a self-employed work-at-home mum. I know a lot of the pros and cons first hand and each and every one of those mums struggles. No one has it anywhere near easy, especially if we are not supporting one another.

The most important thing about being a good mum is making sure your own mental health and happiness is as tip-top as it can be. Personally, I have always felt a very strong need to work, and engage with my passions outside of being a parent. That in itself causes problems in my confused little head.

You see for me to be happy I cannot be a full-time mum. I have nothing but respect for those who do that job but for my children to see and get to know the real me, I need to concentrate on my own dreams too and not just theirs. But one of the hardest things about working is that I often feel like I am spreading myself so thin that I am failing at everything. I'm not a good enough mum, wife, friend or worker.

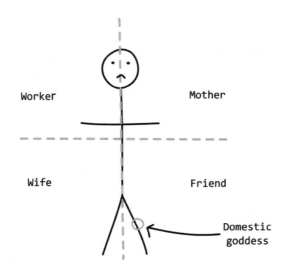

There is also a domestic goddess spot somewhere above my left knee, it's small, neglected and keeps whispering to me to make apple pies. Never gonna happen.

I also wonder if I'm a bad mum because I look forward to having time away from my boys on the days that I'm working, and the stupidest thing of all is that during the time I am supposed to be appreciating being away from them, I just end up missing them instead.

That is the great brain-fuck of parenthood.

The need to escape, the guilt, the worry, the constant questioning that you are not doing a good enough job. How is anyone supposed to make sense of it all?

On the days that I am home I feel like I should be making it up to them by being the BEST MUM EVER.

But that, um, never happens, because it always seems like I'm hitting my head against a brick wall. I get tired of the lack of cooperation and unwillingness to do anything that isn't considered fun. I get bored of my own voice repeating the same requests thirty-seven times and still being ignored.

I feel disappointed in myself for shouting too much (again) even when my head is telling me I shouldn't. TBH if someone could just invent self-applying kids' shoes that alone would help massively!

Sometimes I think that as parents we put too much pressure on ourselves to be perfect. But we are only human, we don't have infinite patience, we can't always say the right thing. We have to accept that when we have so many roles and so many bosses (some harsher than others), it's inevitable that we are going to mess up.

But in our own ways we reassure our children that we are their constant and that they are loved. Whether that's whiling away afternoons at the park or books and cuddles after a day at the office. The routines we figure out provide children with the security they need, regardless of how long we are with or without them.

I'm not saying that I have things completely figured out, in fact sometimes I feel like I'm dropping plates left, right and centre . . .

But in five seconds flat two beautiful faces,
running to see me after a long day away, can make
those smashed plates seem a whole lot less
important.

It's called precision timing.

You see I'm not always there for them, and even
when I am sometimes I suck at parenting them.
But sometimes their dad sucks too . . . and hey
even the kids themselves suck quite a lot of the
time. And sometimes or often, depending on the
day, we all roll around in a great big ball of
suckiness together. But it matters not because

we love each other, and love always* overrides
suckiness.

So even though I've not quite worked out how to
have it all (and I'm still messing a whole lot of
it up) I can see that what we've got is good
enough.

*at least 97% of the time.

'LET IT POO!'

I was reluctant to write a chapter about poo (for obvious reasons) but when you are a parent to young children there really are no two ways about it - poo, and wee for that matter, are massive parts of your lives. My kids are obsessed and it often feels like we can talk about nothing else:

Me: What would you like for dinner?

Little Bro: Poo!

Big Bro: Ha ha and wee!

Little Bro: POO AND WEE!

Big Bro: Farts and poos and wees and bum bums!

Me: I was thinking more along the lines of some actual food?

Little Bro: Stinky bum bum farts!

Big Bro: Disgusting massive poos and wee to drink and lots of smelly farts all around!

Me: Okaaaaaay.

(This can go on for ages but you get my drift . . . one day I might actually serve them up what they asked for and see how much they like it.)

Anyway it doesn't stop there. Little Bro actually calls me 'Mummy Poo' at the moment, which is . . . endearing, and one of their current favourite pastimes is to change the words of songs to incorporate bodily excretions . . .

Kind of funny when it actually works right? Yeh. Kinda.

With all this interest in poo you might have thought potty-training would have been easy. Well . . . not exactly. Neither of mine ever showed any interest in ditching nappies, I've seen friends' children self-train with the excitement of getting fancy knickers. But mine? Nuh uh.

I introduced a potty at around the age of two and followed advice that you should frequently ask if they want to use it and not push until they were ready. The problem was that months and months passed and the answer was always 'NO!' I guess, why would you interrupt your game of grabbing handfuls of hair out of the cat to go to the toilet when it could be someone else's problem? (RIP Pickle, God rest her soul.)

When Big Bro was pushing two and three-quarters I'd had enough and decided we needed to bite the bullet. Unfortunately by that point I also had a twelve-week-old breastfed baby to contend with. Oh kids can be all sorts of clever . . .

We potty-trained Little Bro at a similar age and his party trick was pissing on the floor and then jumping up and down in it like Peppa Pig on speed.

Everywon likes jumpin wee wee puddles!

Except they don't though do they? The point is that normal people don't.

But I swear you reach a new level of parenthood low when you fish a poo out of the bath with your bare hands or catch yourself standing over a potty cheerleading someone else on to take a shit.

*In the above illustration, Mummy demonstrates
how little dignity she has left since
having kids.*

Both times I potty-trained, the main arsenal in my
weaponry was chocolate buttons – which involved
double the bribes the second time round because
you can hardly give one child chocolate buttons
and not the other one right? Therefore Big Bro
took a very healthy interest in his younger
brother's bladder and bowel movements. On one
particular occasion when Little Bro did a massive
poo on the living room floor his first question
was . . .

Sorry kiddo the answer is sweet FA, unless you count the wine Mummy is going to neck later on.

Anyway, you will be glad to hear that these days we are a nappy-free household! The one advantage of waiting until they were slightly older, and also them both being very keen on chocolate buttons, was they were relatively straightforward to crack. Although even now they both occasionally piss themselves when they are too busy playing to bother with the responsibility of their own bladders. Then there is the matter of bum-wiping. When both me and his dad are at home Big Bro likes to pick who will get the honour, like it's a highly coveted prize.

'Right, I'm going to do a poo and when I've finished I will choose you or Daddy to come up and wipe my bum. I will shout out whose name it is when I'm done. OK?'

Oh pick me, pick me!

They also both like to give me a blow-by-blow account of their toileting process . . . 'It's coming. It's coming. It's a big one! Mummy I love yooooouuu! You are the best mummy eveeeeeeeeer!'

Emotional stuff huh?

Then when it's done they like to take a moment to look down the toilet and describe what sort of animal or vehicle it most looks like.

OOH Come and see! This one looks like a penguin!

No. I'm OK. I trust you.

When did having a poo become such a social
occasion, such a conversational opportunity?
Surely it should be a solitary affair. A moment to
collect your thoughts and ponder life.
I mourn the days I took it for granted and would
give anything for the opportunity to have an
uninterrupted shit now. It's the simple stuff eh?

Never gonna happen . . .

TAKE TWO

1st Kid...

> Mmm do you like avocado and sweet potato mash?

2nd Kid...

> Mmm do you like Toffee Crisps?

When Big Bro was very little I remember thinking 'Why and what the hell do people have more than one child for?!' I couldn't work out what the selling point was when so much of it was just shit (literally).

However, when he was a year and a bit old, he became easier and really rather adorable, so it suddenly seemed like a good idea. One is such a cute age huh? It's also quite far away from the newborn days so you tend to look back on that time more favourably and say stuff like 'Oh it wasn't that bad' and 'It was quite lovely really.' WARNING: THIS IS WHAT CHILDREN DO TO TRICK YOU!

But you know, we always wanted more than one and thinking back . . . it wasn't that bad and it was quite lovely really (DOH!). Anyway, long story short, those thoughts happened, so did the biology stuff and a couple of months later I was retching away in bushes again.

One thing I noticed about doing it all over again was that you pay way less attention to your pregnancy. The first time round I pored over my 'watch your foetus grow day-by-day' book. I knew its exact size and what sort of physical developments it was going through.

Second time round? Not a fricking clue. So it can be a bit awkward when people ask you complicated questions like . . .

'Oh baby's growing nicely then. How many weeks are you now?'

If you can remember what trimester you are in, well done, if not, then I suggest you compose your reply by picking a fruit or vegetable and accessorising it with some bodily features. For example:

'Yeh it's growing real good. It's like an avocado with eyelashes. Or fingernails. Or something.'

Whatever. No one really gives a shit do they?

Feel free to make the above pic a screensaver on your phone. It's 100% effective as a means of contraception. As in it makes you not want to have sex again. Ever.

Anyway, after what feels like about five minutes you will suddenly realise you are about to have a baby and freak out. Probably enhanced by the fact that the cutesy one-year-old who made you think another child was a good idea is now a bloody nightmare of a two-year-old. I did not sign up for that but it was too late now.

From the get-go everything is oh so different the second time round . . .

First kid – Arriving home from hospital you retire to the sofa for a well-deserved nap.
Second kid – Arriving home from hospital you are guilt-tripped into playing incredibly tedious games of Fireman Sam with your toddler while simultaneously trying to breastfeed your newborn while simultaneously trying not to fall asleep and/or lose your fricking mind.

First kid – You are inundated with presents and visitors, love, lasagne and promises of babysitting.
Second kid – Where the frick is everybody?! Newsflash: no one cares.

First kid – Ahhh a wardrobe full of pristine outfits spun from organic llama hair – washed, ironed and folded.
Second kid – Shit-stained onesies.

First kid – You take ninety-seven photos per day with the DSLR and meticulously complete a baby milestones book.

Second kid – Errr there's a photo up on Instagram I think? Someone else pointed out their first tooth.

First kid – A well-devised feeding and nap schedule.
Second kid – Feeding and napping can just happen whenever the toddler isn't being a total arsehole.

First kid – Oh my God! Oh my God! Baby has sniffles and can't breathe! Quick, get down the A&E.
Second kid – Oops a limb has fallen off. Never mind just stick it back on.

First kid – Sterilise like a bitch.
Second kid – Adopt the three-second rule.

First kid – Carefully selected age-appropriate TV with some nice singing and moralistic tales.
Second kid – Just whatever the others one's watching really. A bit of killing and violence never hurt anybody right?

First kid – Lovingly prepared organic home-cooked meals.
Second kid – As long as you lick the salt off the chips at Maccie D's it'll be fine.

First kid – Baby has lots of friends due to a jam-packed schedule of classes and playgroups.
Second kid – No friends of their own cos they just get dragged about wherever the older one is going.

First kid – An extravagant first birthday party, with handmade bunting, watermelon sculptures, a champagne cascade, real-fire-breathing dragons and surprise celebrity visit from Iggle Piggle and his slutty BFF Upsy Daisy.

Second kid – Um . . . can't be fucked.

Reading these through, I realise you probably feel a bit like . . . oh dear poor neglected second-born children *sad face*. But the overriding theme isn't one of neglect, it's not even really one of a parent who just has less time; a lot of it boils down to a parent who has just learnt how to parent and therefore not stress over all of the minors.

Sure having a newborn AND a (shall we say wilful?) small child to factor into things should have been a lot harder, and in many physical ways it was – there were two people to cart around, two lots of stuff, two bladders to take care of, two lots of very different needs. I had fewer hands available and needed more patience – and more gin!

But I knew what I was doing (mostly) and that, that alone, makes the shift from one to two much less scary than from zero to one. I've heard people say that two to three is easier still but I'll just have to trust them on that as I have no intention of finding out myself. Until I see a tiny ickle baby and then I'm all like . . .

But for now we have two and I'm happy with two. The overriding selling point and clincher of the deal for having a second in the first place was for Big Bro. This concept of a much-adored sibling for him was oh so sweet, someone to play with, someone to confide in . . . a friend for life!

However, as with many of my parenting experiences, it didn't go exactly as planned and Big Bro took an immediate dislike to our brand new addition. I see pictures pop up on Facebook all the time of the cute moments when big brothers and sisters meet their siblings for the first time – there was NONE of that at ours. The only photos we have of them together in the early days involved leaning Little Bro against Big Bro's arm when he was utterly transfixed by the iPad and therefore less likely to shove him away.

As they grew it transpired that there are people who have kids who get on and look out for each other, and then there are people who have kids where the best possible scenario is that they are completely ignoring each other at separate ends of the room. We fell into the latter camp – YAY!

Although they are friendlier these days, at times it still feels like I can't leave them alone for five seconds without a full-on war breaking out. Here are a few of the things that they regularly argue about while I am trying to make tea/hang the washing up/make an important phone call:

I. 'That's mine!'-related arguments.

Doesn't matter what it is, some screwed-up bit of an old *CBeebies* magazine that was plucked out of the bin, whatever, if it was once yours and someone else is now touching it then that is grounds to go apeshit until you get it back.

Then when you get it back you can immediately discard it because you never REALLY wanted it in the first place. Obviously.

This also extends to feeling threatened by another person because they are LOOKING (gasps) at something you are playing with.

2. TV-related arguments.

Including – 'He's watched two episodes of his programme and I've only watched one of mine', 'He's standing in front of the TV and I can't see', 'He turned my programme off and it wasn't finished yet', 'He is shouting and I can't hear', etc. etc.

Even if I find something they are both happy to watch and I've managed to get them to sit down sensibly on the sofa, we get . . .

3. Proximity-related arguments.

If I sit with them to try and keep the peace then they fight over me like a piece of meat ...

4. 'Me first!'-related arguments.

I have (mostly) become a bit of a pro at avoidance techniques on this one. It's like silver service round ours – I make sure I place their food and drinks and snacks on the table at EXACTLY the same time.

I can do nothing to quell the storm of the 'who gets taken out of the car first' arguments though, but to be fair on them it is a biggie. Who wouldn't fight tooth and nail for the much coveted prize of getting to stand on the pavement for an extra ten seconds . . .? Exactly.

(Please excuse the state of my car.)

5. Cutlery-related arguments.

I find this one frustrating because I often get it wrong, through no fault of my own but because the favourite spoons, plates and other very similar, yet also incredibly different, tableware preferences seem to change on a daily basis.

I doubt his argument would stack up very well in a courtroom . . .

Me: I present to the courtroom Exhibit A, a document dated err YESTERDAY stating that the defendant's 'special spoon' (N.B not to be pronounced 'soon') is the one with the orange handle with a chip at the top. Is that your name there alongside the crude drawing of Raphael from the Ninja Turtles?

Big Bro: Oh yeh Raf he's my favourite.

Me: Then I put it to you that the spoon your brother is currently holding is not your favourite and you are only saying it is to wind him up!

audible gasps from the gallery

Me: So I ask you this – IS YOUR FAVOURITE SPOON THE ORANGE CHIPPED SPOON OR THE YELLOW WINNIE THE POOH SPOON?!?!?!

Big Bro (head hung in shame): It's the orange one with the chip.

Me: I rest my case.

Siblings eh, who'd have 'em?!

BEDTIME FUCKWITTERY

Daytime Kid	Night-time Kid
Thinks water is disgusting	Develops an unquenchable thirst
Pisses pants	Makes excessive trips to toilet
Only ever talks about farts	Wants to debate the big bang theory
Drop kicks teddies	Needs 27 'special friends' in bed
Thinks I am a stupid poo head	Loves me to the moon and back
Frequently tries to kill self	Too worried about death to sleep

Big Bro wishes he didn't have to waste his life having to sleep because it is 'too long and too boring'. When he is seventeen I am going to remind him of this by going into his room at 6 a.m. and banging pans together next to his head.

Let me be honest with you. I guess you are meant to enjoy putting your kids to bed – such a special time huh? Reading stories, cuddling, talking about your day . . . well sorry but I mostly just hate it. Often it seems like the final 'fuck you' after a hard day.

However, now I am an *ahem* experienced parent with over six years on the job, we have pretty much perfected the process so I thought I'd share our relaxing *ahem* bedtime routine . . .

1. **TV and milk** – At about 6 p.m. we begin winding down. The process starts with an argument over what we should watch on TV (as per the previous chapter), followed by an argument that the milk should be milkshake and not just milk and ends in a WWF-style wrestling match in which one child lies on the sofa while the other child jumps from the coffee table and lands on top of them. It's approximately a 50:50 laughter-to-tears ratio, which sets things off beautifully.

2. A lovely bath – Next up we go through a two-stage FML objection to bath time.

1. I don't want to get in the bath!

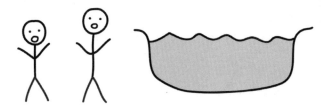

2. I don't want to get out of the bath!

3. Brushing teeth – We are all feeling super chilled now so it's time to clean our teeth; this is one of my favourite parts as it puts Little Bro into a RAGE that requires physical restraint.

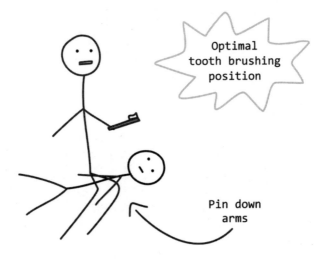

4. Story time – Everyone loves a nice snuggle with a good book before bed don't they?!

The fantasy . . .

The reality . . .

5. **Lights out and general fuckwittery** – Here commence the 137 reasons why Big Bro cannot go to sleep yet (see the chart at the start of this chapter on page 189 as a quick reference guide). As I write this he has just got out of bed for his second poo that is conveniently stuck and won't come out. That he prefers to be on a cold toilet, pretending to take a dump, rather than be in a warm cosy bed says everything you need to know about kids. Bat. Shit. Crazy.

6. **Waiting in the dark for an hour** – Little Bro needs one of us to stay in the room with him until he falls asleep. When I say 'needs' it's more of a prevention thing because if you leave him alone he just gets out of bed and runs about upstairs shrieking like a deranged guinea pig.

At least I get to lie on the floor and look up ~~celebrity gossip~~ news articles on my phone so it's not all bad.

7. **Alcohol** – Number seven is actually the only relaxing part of the relaxing bedtime routine. Or at least it should be, but sadly the sound of the sweet liquid hitting the bottom of the glass is often interrupted by . . .

8. **Additional fuckwittery** – Also known as 'I've got something really, really important to tell you!'

SILENT SCREAM

But eventually, eventually they always give in. Hurrah that's it until morning! UNLESS you are stuck with a toddler who has become a right pain in the arse about staying in his own bed.

People don't talk that much about these types of issues do they? You always hear about baby sleep and how much sympathy people have for new mums but to me those newborn days seem almost preferable, because at least babies don't kick you in the head and demand you make them jam on toast while doing an impression of a cat at 2.45 a.m.

If you were to ask me 'How are your kids at sleeping?' I would say 'Hmm OK. Not great, but OK-ish . . . you know, depending on the day. Actually. Often. A bit crap.'

If they both sleep through and neither one gets up until 6 a.m. then that is a big win. I cannot remember the last time this happened. At the minute our main problem is Little Bro's habit of appearing in our room and scaring the crap out of us in the middle of the night (I say us but TBH J is blessed with the gift of being a deep sleeper so remains mostly unaware).

I know we should probably make some attempt to teach him to sleep in his own bed, take him back to his room quietly and quickly, be consistent bla bla bla but OH THE TIRED. It's always too tempting to just go with the quickest win.

(Although even I've never made jam on toast at 2.45 a.m. while pretending to be a cat.*)

Anyway, the ideal scenario is that he gets into our bed and goes back to sleep immediately. It happens. Occasionally.

Unfortunately we are also met with other, less preferable, outcomes. For example sometimes he becomes **Chatty Kid** . . .

Other times he is **Invasive Kid** and winds down by spending thirty minutes or so poking or prodding me . . .

And **Cute Kid** ups the game with clever distraction techniques (he can't say love properly yet and pronounces it lush *heart melts*) . . .

Did you notice the father sleeping through it all?
Not for long! **Are You Sure He's Not On Acid
Kid** will soon see to that . . .

Often he decides to play **Hungry Kid,** suddenly demanding to eat the meal he outright refused to even try at dinnertime . . .

All of those scenarios are better than dealing with **Angry Kid.** No one is really sure why **Angry Kid** is angry, even **Angry Kid** himself does not know. He just picks a ridiculous and random thing to get pissed off about and runs with it (while ripping the covers off everybody) . . .

He knows full well that he doesn't even have yellow wellies.

If we are very unfortunate we might have to deal with **Hangry Kid,** a horrible combination of the previous two, basically meaning we are totally screwed . . .

In most cases **Hangry Kid** also turns into **I'm Going to Hit Everybody Until Someone Gives Me Their Space In The Bed Kid** . . .

But I've saved the best for last. Nothing, no one and no type of night-time bed invader is more terrifying than **Thinks It's Already Daytime Kid** . . .

shudders

However, the good news is that most of the time we are able to persuade our little one back into a peaceful slumber. Unfortunately by that time it's often around 5.35 a.m. and DAMN IT just as I'm about to drift back off, I remember – we have another kid who likes to get up before the crack of dawn . . .

Gimme a newborn any day.

*At least 87% sure I've never done it . . .

P.S. Yes we do have a Gro-Clock and no it doesn't work. They say waiting for the sun to come on is too boring and/or unplug it. If I'm honest though, I have to give credit to anyone who refuses to be dictated to by an electrical appliance with a stupid smug smiley face.

THE CHICKENPOX DIARIES

Sick kids are so confusing. On the one hand you look at your poor ill child lying desolate on the sofa and you want to cuddle them, mop their brow and take all the pain away. And on the other hand you want to stand them up, put their shoes on and say 'Stop inconveniencing me!'

Oh come on, I've seen the parents outside the nursery gates dosing their kids up with Calpol before they send them in! It's just that kids always seem to get sick when you have a really important deadline or an incredibly rare child-free afternoon to enjoy, don't they? And if you kept your kid at home every time they had a sniffle there would never be anyone at nursery. I'm surprised the staff are even able to tell the kids apart considering so many of them have their whole faces covered in snot.

But there is no getting around the dreaded chicken-pox. The appearance of small red bumps means no nursery. Worse than that . . . It means quarantine. I kept a diary to document the horror when it happened to us, let me share it with you now . . .

Day 1
Text from J . . .

(We sometimes text using only emojis and no words because it is honestly quite funny but I realise it does sound a bit sad if you say it out loud and maybe even worse if you write it down.)

Anyway, turns out he means that Little Bro has chickenpox, tenuous at best. Never mind, I am in London seeing friends. Not my problem.

Day 2
Who cares? I'm in LONDON still! :)

Day 3 - Subtitle: THE DAY OF NO SLEEP
Back home now and Little Bro seems mostly OK in himself. That is until bedtime when he decides to forgo sleep in lieu of thrashing about like a wild animal.

The only thing that calms him down is Fireman Sam. How long do you think a toddler would be able to stay up watching Netflix?

Yes I was surprised too.

Day 4

We all felt rather shaky and sick as a result of the sleep deprivation and overexposure to the Dilys, Trevor and Station Officer Steele love triangle.

To ensure we got a better night J went to the pharmacy to try and hit them up for some of the good stuff.

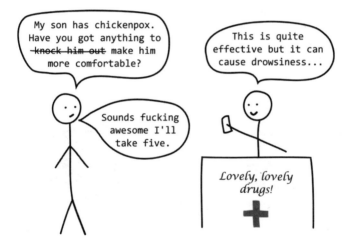

Day 5
They worked – had an amazing seven-hour sleep! I
never sleep for that long so I feel strange . . .
almost a bit . . . enthusiastic? Or something.

Luckily the boy is also much better. Although now
he wants to go out and do normal stuff but we can't
because he is still infectious. I intermittently
throw Play-Doh, chocolate and Calpol at him and try
to avoid getting cracked over the back of the head
with pieces of train track.

Can't quite work out whether I prefer the sick
version of him or the well one.

Gin.

Day 6
Getting bored now.

Spent a high proportion of the day analysing scab
progression and trying not to pick them.

I found that another fun activity to do is to calculate
the amount you have paid nursery in the last month Vs.
the number of sessions that were physically attended.
You can then work out the actual cost per session.

Ours was £136.05!

Vomits

Day 7

Very bored and in desperate need of conversation.

Feel like I might be turning into one of those nutters who ask Google questions like it's an actual real live person.

Google – do you think nurseries keep vials of infectious diseases in secret underground laboratories in order to maximise profits? Do you like my new trainers? What are you having for lunch?

Started work on my political manifesto. It needs fleshing out but I think I made good progress.

Monster Munch

4 Lyf

A fun day.

Day 8

We are now SCABBED OVER! Took Little Bro back to nursery but was very nervous that the thieving bastards would try and refuse him.

Luckily they seemed to have hit their quota of sick kids for the day.

Got on with trying to do a week's worth of work in one day. Failed.

Day 9

Hurrah! We can now get out and about again, which is sooooo nice (mostly).

Day 10

Everyone is much better, except me. I am a bit stressed out as I have so much to do and so little time to do it.

When I get tired and stressed I have a tendency to start crying at small things. For example realising that there is only one Nespresso capsule left in the pot. TEARS.

Actually that was a large thing.

I can face most things in life but not without coffee . . .

Then I remember . . .

We have Amazon Prime!

And I know, I just know that everything is going to be OK . . .

But I was an idiot, of course, because a week later Big Bro caught it and we went through the whole trauma again. But none of that, nor the sickness bugs, the ear infections or the coughs and colds, are a patch on being sick yourself while looking after well children.

The problem here is that small children and babies are incredibly selfish and do not give a frick about your own suffering. It's not their fault – we are all born that way. Slowly over the course of time they learn that if they want to fit in and be liked then they must consider the feelings of others. But I reckon a lot of adults would remain 100% selfish if they weren't so scared of having no friends. I hate sharing my crisps but I do it because I don't want people to think I'm a cow (when I get really old I'm going to start being selfish again because FUCK EVERYBODY else when you are about to die).

Anyway, I do try to ask my kids to be kind and nice to me when I'm poorly but there is very little point because ultimately they don't care . . .

Could you be a little less noisy please? Mummy's got a headache.

NO.

Could you stop jumping on me please? Because I think I'm about to vomit . . .

NO.

Could you get me a glass of water please? I'm feeling weak and dehydrated . . .

NO.

I mean I could be dying. I could be literally dead on the floor and they would only be feeling inconvenienced by the late arrival of their snacks . . .

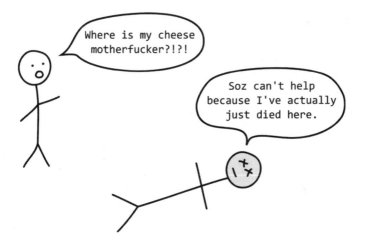

I'M STILL HERE, I'M STILL ME

Before Kids

After Kids

Carefree radiance

Non-dead eyes

Waistline

Basically an evil witch

Help! I'm missing. Recently I'm sure I was like twenty-five or something?! But now when I look in the mirror it's not my face that's looking back but someone older. Much older. I now have wrinkles, a permanent expression of irritation and it hurts (like literally in my back when I bend over).

My children have aged me and it's no mystery why. Any beauty advice will tell you that aside from ridiculously expensive face creams you need sleep, water and a trendy raw-food diet to stay youthful-looking. Annoyingly, no sleep, large glasses of Sauvignon Blanc and eating the remnants of discarded fish fingers off the floor has the opposite effect.

I look at my body, the tummy that grew two babies, the boobs that expanded with milk to feed them and then deflated and never exactly returned (fuckers), the thighs that have grown increasingly wibbly over the years. My nail varnish is currently chipped and will likely stay that way for at least a week until I actually bother to remove it and my make-up is limited to concealer that partially hides my dark circles.

I am wearing what I usually wear, which is skinny jeans and a simple tee. I look neither fashionable nor unfashionable. I look just like most other mums I guess . . .

BUT this is not good enough I am told. I am losing my identity to generic 'mumdom' and I need help! Is it just me or does anyone else feel like screaming into the abyss every time they read a magazine article about how to be less 'mumsy'? You see we are constantly bombarded with messages in the media that looking like, or being perceived as, a mum is just not that palatable. What I want to know is, when did being a mum become something to be ashamed of?

Apparently we should wipe away all of the physical signs of the amazing job our bodies have done and prioritise getting back into bikinis, we should avoid wearing 'mumiforms' (because yes a mum uniform is a real thing now even though it's stripy tops, parkas and Converse which incidentally are just normal people clothes that everybody wears, yet only mums get the flak for) and we should get some new hobbies to stop us banging on about our kids so much – learn a language, train to be a Pilates instructor, take up cake decorating – the choice is yours!

And what about the dads? Despite them often being in a very similar predicament, why are they not under so much pressure to avoid slipping into 'daddom' by appearing to be 'dadsy' in their boring 'dadiforms'? Oh yeh, because it's just more sexist bullshit that's dumped on women to convince them that spending money on stuff they don't need would make them feel more worthwhile.

Maybe this would actually make us all feel more worthwhile . . .

I don't know, maybe I'm just finding it hard because I've got a lot on my plate right now . . .

'Perhaps a mindfulness course would help?' suggests a chilled-out parenting expert with lovely shiny hair.

No. Mindfulness can fuck off!

There is no denying that I don't look as good as I could do any more and I no longer have as much exciting news to share but hey there is one big problem standing in my way you shiny-haired parenting experts, and I apologise for shouting here but . . .

I HAVE NO FRICKING TIME FOR MYSELF!

Yeh – the complete lack of time your average mum (or dad) actually has. For me a lack of 'me time' has certainly been one of the hardest things to adjust to. A lot of the advice you read about parenthood says . . .

> *'Be sure to remember to make time for you –*
> *you are no good to anyone else if you don't*
> *take care of yourself first.'*

It's certainly not bad advice, in fact it's solid gold advice but what I want to know is how do you 'make' time, because as far as I can see time is either there or it's not. Most of the time it's simply not, and even Jamie Oliver doesn't have the recipe.

So come on, where do I find this elusive 'me time'?

In the daytime I'm either working or keeping small people alive so it can't be then – what about the evenings? One of the first things I do after putting the kids to bed is tidy up, and when I say tidy I mean do anal stuff like reorganise the play kitchen that they never play with and setting up a wooden cooked breakfast in the frying pan. Is that this mysterious thing they call 'me time'?

Maybe 'me time' happens when I get to finally plop down on the sofa and watch twenty minutes of *The Lego Batman Movie*, which I have already seen 137 times, before I finally realise and turn the blasted thing off (TBH it's an improvement on The Bedtime Hour hold screen. I think).

It's 9 p.m. now. Does cooking dinner count as 'me time'? Does eating dinner count as 'me time'? Does washing up? Does trying to file my tax return while half-watching *Location, Location, Location*? Does the five hours' sleep I'll get when I finally collapse into bed?

I wondered . . . have any other parents had luck in finding it?

Becky (forty-one) 'The other day I got to empty the dishwasher without someone hanging off my leg and it set me up for the whole week.'

Lucy (thirty-three) 'I like reading bitchy comments on the *Daily Mail* website while I'm pretending to watch Mr Tumble.'

Louise (twenty-nine) 'I had my wisdom teeth taken out in day surgery. I got to read *Glamour* magazine and eat a whole strawberry yoghurt to myself, it was epic.'

Dave (thirty-seven) 'If I can have a poo in peace then I'm happy.'

It seems I am not alone.

My happy place is a long hot bubble bath with the weekend supplements. The problem is that it often culminates in one or both children jumping in to join me and the feelings of 'Zen' are well and truly lost as I find myself locked in a conversation about why I don't have a willy . . .

The magazines would have us believe that all of our problems would be fixed by sending us off to sit about on sunloungers in expensive spas. Oh dear look at the poor old downtrodden mummy, never has enough time for herself, boo hoo, quick give her a mini manicure and a dip in the Jacuzzi and then send her back to her crappy life.

Don't get me wrong, I'd never turn down a trip to the spa - it's just that I don't like the distinction between 'me time' being some sort of holy grail and normal life being, well . . . shit. Plus I've never been able to relax under pressure anyway . . .

The answer to feeling more like myself is not via disassociation from my children in terms of the things I do or the way I look. I'm not going to be ashamed of their existence because some silly bint in a magazine tells me so. Err hello, I know they are annoying, believe me, but I also kind of like them!

Stand 3 metres away please. I want people to look at my new handbag - not you!

It's just that there is not a lot of 'me time' when you have young children, dem's da breaks. What we have now is 'us time' because we come as a package deal. And that's OK because I love being a mum and I am certainly not embarrassed if people perceive me as one.

So I think my point here is, dress however the hell you like, whether that's 'like a mum' or like a high-fashion catwalk model, do whatever you like, take an evening course in ancient hieroglyphics if you can find the time/brain cells or just lounge about on the sofa drinking wine like the rest of us. Go to the gym because it makes you feel good about yourself or embrace your mum tum and stretchmarks and all the wonderfulness they have brought you.

Enjoy the snippets of time you get to yourself if you are able to find them, and don't sweat it if you can't. You'll get that time back eventually – for now you'll just have to grab your kicks wherever you can . . .

Sainsbury's Local

Parenthood: When nipping out for some milk alone... feels like a trip to the spa!

P.S. I always let my boys in when I'm having a bath.

P.P.S. I secretly enjoy it.

P.P.P.S. I'd just like to make it abundantly clear that I'd still really REALLY like to go on a spa break, but just because I'm a good person and I deserve it, not because it's some sort of consolation prize.

WE'RE ALL GOING ON A SUMMER HELLIDAY

Helliday (noun).
Definition: Same old shit, different location:

'Sarah's helliday cost her 2 grand and the remainder
 of her sanity.'
'Fred enjoys hellidays as much standing on Lego.'
'Happy hellidays (you bloody idiots).'

I'm not saying holidays aren't fun once you have
kids, I'm just saying they are a bit err . . . less
fun? Sometimes I think – considering packing – is
it even worth going at all?

You see I used to adore the pre-holiday prep of
yesteryear but these days instead of hunting down
the perfect shimmery suntan cream I am more likely
to be panic-buying kids' Crocs on eBay. It got me

thinking about how different holidays are now that
we have children . . .

1. Planning and preparations

Researching the destination
- Before kids: Look up nice bars, restaurants and
  cultural places of interest to visit.
- After kids: That place you booked because it
  said it was 'child friendly' and had decent
  Wi-Fi? Now look up what country it's actually
  in. Then look up the nearest A&E.

Entertainment
- Before kids: Download some new music and order
  three books from Amazon for relaxing by the
  pool.
- After kids: Charge the iPad to within an inch
  of its life and fill it with an abundance of
  irritating crap. Don't bother with anything for
  yourself because your entertainment will
  consist purely of making sure your kids don't
  drown.

Pampering
- Before kids: Allocate the evening before for
  a beautifying session. Have a nice bath,
  shave legs, paint toes, apply fake tan.
  RELAX.

- After kids: Allocate the evening before to have a fight about who was meant to book the airport parking (not me!) before angrily clipping your toenails and butchering your legs with a manky blunt razor.

Packing
- Before kids: Select daytime outfits AND evening outfits. Take double the amount of clothes that it is actually possible to wear including numerous pairs of shoes with varying heel heights.
- After kids: Fill up one whole suitcase with nappies, factor 50 sun cream and Calpol and fill up the rest with kids' clothes, kids' spare clothes, blow-up items, plastic beach crap, blackout blinds, special cups and twenty-six absolutely vital toys that cannot possibly be left behind. Then cram three £5 dresses from Primark, your trusty five-year-old bikini and some multi-purpose daytime/evening flip-flops in the suitcase least likely to burst while muttering 'What's the fucking point?' at regular intervals.

Getting to the airport
- Before kids: Chat excitedly in the car on the way to the airport and arrive feeling calm and excited about your trip.

- After kids: Cry. Don't talk unless it's in swear words. Intermittently throw sweets into the back of the car to appease your overtired offspring who decided to sleep past 5 a.m. on the ONE DAY that you needed to leave the house at 5 a.m. Arrive at the airport on the brink of divorce covered in a ridiculous quantity of children, luggage, car seats and buggies, looking like a goddam camel. Feel glad that at airports it's socially acceptable to drink 24/7 and have a pint with your McDonald's breakfast.

2. Travel

ARGHHGHGGHGGHH. Kids on a plane. Like snakes on a plane but WAY scarier. Unfortunately to go on holiday you also have to get there and that might involve getting on a plane to the furthest destination you dared book. Four hours is my upper limit, respect to all those who have done more.

Last time we went on holiday with our kids we flipped a coin for who got to sit next to Big Bro Vs. Little Bro. You see it turns out five-year-olds are pretty awesome to sit next to on planes – seeing their excitement and wonder at the world has got to be one of the best bits of parenting. Even if they do end up making you feel pretty stupid . . .

In comparison, sitting next to a toddler on a plane is um . . . interesting?! Actually sorry, it just sucks.

I'd rather take the difficult questions . . .

. . . over being sat next to a person who only wants to do one of three incredibly irritating things.

1.	2.	3.
I likey openy closey window!	I likey push my buttons!	I likey bangy my tray!

Unfortunately the cabin crew don't particularly like being repeatedly summoned over by a toddler who just wants to blow raspberries in their faces; and fellow passengers don't particularly like the headaches induced by a window and/or dinner tray being constantly punched.

It was a difficult one to deal with though because if he was doing one of his preferred activities he was happy, and if he was being prevented from doing so, then he was audibly not happy. So it was a lose/lose situation because everyone just wanted him to sit quietly in his seat not touching anything, which was never going to happen.

So we had a lot of very different air travel experiences going on – some of the best bits of parenting, some of the worst bits of parenting and a whole bunch of miserable-looking bastards who just got unlucky.

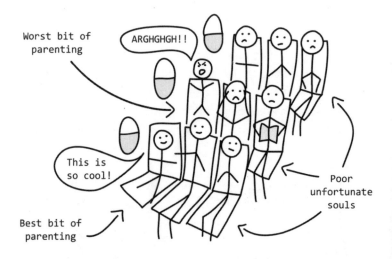

We also had a few other families with young kids around us, which you may assume to be a good thing. We exchanged a couple of those 'OH BLOODY KIDS!' looks but I often found that if their kids were behaving better than mine, then those knowing looks also contained an element of judgey smugness. To be fair, if my kids are behaving better than theirs then that is exactly what I would be feeling too.

So anyway, it was all going a bit fuck fuckity fucksticks. Until . . .

ENTER: The trolley of dreams full of snack packs and alcohol . . .

Oh easyJet you little beauty!

Look at all the things for him to do! Paint the seats with the Laughing Cow dippers, soak the pointless books we bought in pineapple juice, stab us in the legs with those lethally sharp colouring pencils and eat the packet of Nutella with his fingers before wiping his hands through everyone's hair and then just . . . relentlessly headbutting me.

But you go kid, knock yourself out! Do whatever you like, just do it quietly(ish) and leave me to my small bottles of fizz.

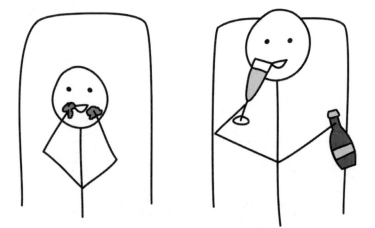

3. The actual 'holiday'

When you arrive (I've trained myself to block out
the transfers) the holiday can begin! Well, that
is once you've tested the Wi-Fi connection because
let's face it, it won't be a holiday for anyone if
your kids can't watch DisneyCollectorBR opening
Kinder Eggs on YouTube.

The next thing to do is hit the pool! My favourite
pre-kid holidays were all-inclusive jaunts to the
Caribbean with my friend Jane. We would basically
while away the hours working our way through the
cocktail menus at the swim-up bar. Two Cuba libres,
two banana mamas and two coco locos please! And
that's just for me. For breakfast. God it was ace.

When you have kids you just spend time at the pool catching them as they jump in off the edge (how do they not get tired of this?) and arguing about whose turn it is to sort out a shit-filled swim nappy (bleak).

Lunch won't involve leisurely sampling the local cuisine with an ice-cold beer, but rather just going anywhere that serves chicken nuggets. Your evening entertainment could include all sorts of exciting things: going to see a horrific family entertainment show that will involve you agreeing to a disco dancing competition with a large dog/teddy/monkey type thing and losing, or if you were stupid enough to book a family room you could just sit in the bathroom drinking wine from a toothbrush holder while waiting for your kids to finally pass out.

BUT I do have the key to having a relaxing holiday with small people, and that is just accepting that it's not really meant to be relaxing, and realising that life without my little lilo invaders would actually be pretty dull.

Sure, holidays might be a massive stress but they make happy go on my boys' faces and that's good enough for me.

(If that's not good enough for you then I have two words - Kids Club.)

Later on when we get home and spend time looking through the photos we always find ourselves smiling and laughing. People ask us if we had a good time and instead of telling them about the thirty-five-degree-heat mega-tantrum over an inflatable killer whale, we reply 'It was lovely!' and 'Yes, really good thanks!' This is known as 'rosy retrospection', which is a good thing for holiday companies and also the reason why people decide to have multiple children.

ME AND MY SIDEKICKS

I didn't have much self-esteem or confidence growing up. I guess that's the same for a lot of people.

I wanted to be liked, I wanted to fit in, and I cared a lot about what people thought about me. I felt grateful, honoured even, when those I deemed to be better or cooler than me gave me attention.

I worried about the way I looked, that everyone was prettier, cleverer or funnier than me. I felt a little bit lost. I felt a bit like a potato in a sea of more interesting-looking vegetables.

But I don't feel like that now. What's changed? It's not me exactly, I'm still as much of a potato as I always was, but I've started to appreciate my values despite that; potatoes might be common as muck but they are versatile and filling, plus they make chips and everybody loves chips!

Part of that thought process has been about growing older and being more comfortable in my own skin(!) but having kids has changed the way I think most of all.

I was kneeling in front of the mirror a little while back putting make-up on before an evening out and Little Bro was watching me with interest. He asked me what I was doing and if he could put some on too . . .

Whoever knew that the most important life lessons would fall from the mouths of babes? My kids can't see my flaws, they see beauty as it should be seen, from the inside out. So now I'm working hard on that one too.

And it doesn't stop there. When I started thinking about it there are so many ways my kids are enriching my life and making me feel like and be a better potato person.

For example they are teaching me things all the time. Things I took for granted. Things I'd stopped even thinking about. The human body, dinosaurs, photosynthesis (plants - wow you are so clever!) and space - I'm learning it all again ...

It's mind-blowing.

I see things through their eyes, things my own eyes would have skipped past. Things only a child's imagination and creativity would focus on . . .

The world is suddenly so vivid.

I get to act like I'm eight years old again, I get to buy all the really cool stuff I want in the toyshop and pretend it's for the kids – like Screwball Scramble. I get to do fun stuff like going down slides and jumping on bouncy castles. I can eat ice-creams EVERY DAY.

They also keep me grounded, they are refreshingly honest and they are always on hand to cheer me back up when I fail . . .

I've learnt to prioritise and place value on my limited free time. I've given up watching *Hollyoaks* – I wasted years on that shit. I've stopped taking crap off people, doing stuff that I don't want to do and trying to impress people who will never be impressed.

My kids have liberated me.

They are my sidekicks, the little cats who crawl into my lap when I need a cuddle, my confidence builders, my pick-me-uppers, my everythings.

I can be having the shittiest of shitty days, I can be so tired and so cross and so at the end of my tether. But when I tuck Big Bro into bed he makes everything else in life seem so insignificant with a simple sentence, which he continues to mispronounce and I continue to neglect to correct, because I love the way he says it like this more . . .

> You are my best girl in the whole tire world.

There will always be people looking down on me but it matters so much less because I know my boy is always looking up. I am his best girl in the 'whole tire world' and suddenly I can't really think of much else that's important.

(As a final note – just in case anyone has read through these points and thought huh?! A lot of this is wholly contradictory to stuff she has said in previous chapters, for example that children make you look shitter, playing with them is boring and how their relentless questions make your head want to explode, then yes you are right but that's just kids. In fact that's just life. One long series of contradictions and then you die. The end.)

KIDS AND HANGOVERS — BLURGH

Hangovers before...

All alone

Big-Mac

Trashy TV

Hangovers now...

Noisy things

laundry

Cbeebies

I have always liked a good night out! I started going clubbing in an era when bouncers didn't seem to give a shit about letting sixteen-year-olds through the doors. If they ever queried my age, my older sister's birth certificate or a crappy fake

ID would be enough to swing it. When I ask my mum and dad why they would let me out while I was still at school they just said 'Well you would have done it anyway!'

Nights would usually start at my house, because it was closest to town and also my parents didn't mind noisy girls playing TLC on repeat. We would down half-sized bottles of vodka with a dash of Coke and leave wearing outfits that more closely resembled underwear – or actually were underwear. If we were feeling flash we would have 50p in our pockets to put our coats in the cloakroom, but more often than not we had no money and staggered out of the house in crop tops, miniskirts and heels we could barely walk in, in the middle of winter. It was all about looking good (although on reflection we looked horrific) – why let a bit of sleet get in the way eh?

I have so many funny/tragic drunken stories I could probably write an entire book on them alone. *When Gin Goes Bad – The Pre-Child Years*. Or maybe not. However, what would often happen was that at least one of us would end up puking in the gutter before we even got to the club. Totally irresponsible behaviour or a rite of passage?

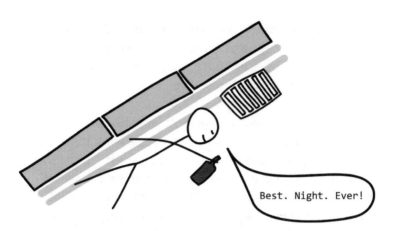

I'll let you decide. But the point is that it didn't matter how drunk you got because you could sleep in until 1 p.m. the next day (do you remember doing that? I couldn't now, even if I had the opportunity). And hangovers, well they just didn't really exist in the same way. Nothing a trip to Maccie D's couldn't fix anyway.

It's a little different these days.

One of the great things about growing older is that you become increasingly level-headed and less inclined to give in to peer pressure. Therefore nights out are an all-round safer affair.

. . . or maybe that's just the case for some people, because for me it's absolute bollocks. If anything I have got worse with age and am a downright liability on the best of occasions.

Of course it always starts out with the best of intentions . . .

It's just a standing joke in our house. J knows that if I stop answering my phone and don't turn up home when I say I will, I am less likely to be dead in a ditch and more likely to be dancing to Justin Bieber on a table in a late-night bar.

I have also been known to be the person on the left but shhh don't tell anyone.

You see I seem to have problems locating that elusive off switch, even more so now that I rarely have a chance to go out. There's a fine line between being slightly merry, lucid and fun and being . . . a total dick.

It's all fun and games at the time though right?
At the time it's perfectly possible to forget that
you have children and/or hideous engagements
planned for the next day.

It is only when you are woken up at 5.30 a.m. by them
jumping up and down on your head after you've only
had two hours' sleep that you remember them, full,
fucking, well. And then there is the crushing
realisation of Daniel's fifth birthday party at funky
wanky shonkey donkey funplex at 11 a.m. to deal with.

KILL ME NOW! God, being an adult really, really
sucks at times.

And even if you have a clear day you can't throw
yourself a self-indulgent pity party like you used
to. No reality TV binge-fest, no stuffing your face
full of crisps while hiding under a blanket, no
crying into a can of Coke while frantically
checking your phone for embarrassing drunken
declarations of love.

Usually in our household we are relatively nice to
each other when one of us is a tad delicate, but

sometimes we are complete bastards because it's
fun (for the one that feels OK) to be mean . . .

In such situations I set to work on my ten-step
programme for dealing with children while
hungover:

1. Play dead.

2. Play dead some more.

3. That's it really. You just hope they will
eventually get bored and leave you alone . . .

Don't rise to the bait. Just keep opting out.
There is plenty of time to start contributing to
life again soon, just not right this moment.

Oh no! Now the other one's showed up . . .

You think it can't get any worse? It can ...

But the problem is that whenever I try and close my eyes, they always spot it. Even if I'm watching some stupid crap with them on Netflix, they keep checking on me to see if I'm paying attention and then trying to prise my eyelids open with their fingertips.

I love my kids always, I like them sometimes, and I want to spend time with them when I'm hungover – never. And that leads to even MORE GUILT to add to my increasing list of woes . . .

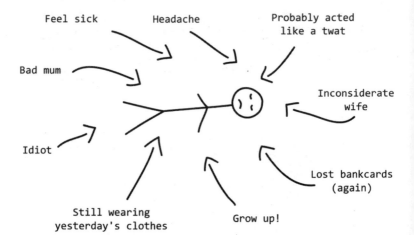

Feel sick
Headache
Probably acted like a twat
Bad mum
Inconsiderate wife
Idiot
Lost bankcards (again)
Still wearing yesterday's clothes
Grow up!

Perhaps I need to get off the floor, leave the house and shock the hangover out of my system? I know – let's go out and visit a National Trust property because I am a grown-up and that is what grown-up people do with their days!

But when we get there I'm not sure any more because it's all a bit bright and colourful and everybody else looks so bloody functional that it's scaring me. People are wandering about talking about lovely flowers and shit and I'm just hiding from small noisy people and trying not to puke into an ornamental fountain.

It's a no-win situation. Whoever invented kids clearly never had a hangover.

(Still worth it though. BRB Justin, love ya!)

YOUR CHILDREN AND THE GENERAL PUBLIC

The thing with kids is that they are mostly OK, if they are doing something that THEY like. The problem is that there are also many things that they don't like doing, things that bring out the worst in them.

Added to your problems is that most of these things involve their exposure to the general public, so you also have to factor in that you are being constantly observed and must therefore remain calm, patient and serene when your toddler kicks off about not being allowed to run wild with a nine-inch kitchen knife in John Lewis.

It's utterly exhausting trying to come across as a good person! Sometimes I just can't wait to get home and be the real me again . . .

Unfortunately though, our lives cannot completely revolve around our offspring. Occasionally we need to get shit done and kids make getting shit done harder x 10,000 (that's an actual scientific fact). Here are a bunch of things that I dislike doing the most:

Errands/Appointments

I hate errands. So boring right? Urgh life and all its admin. Do you know what is worse than errands though? Errands with children. I avoid taking my children on errands at all costs because I HATE ERRANDS WITH CHILDREN SO MUCH!

I think that's clear. I feel slightly better now thank you.

I'm talking about stuff like going to the doctors, getting feet measured for ridiculously overpriced school shoes, 'popping' to the supermarket or queueing up at the post office.

What do all of those things have in common? Waiting time.

My children like to use waiting time to be an absolute bloody nightmare by pulling stuff off shelves, throwing themselves on to the floor because you say they can't pull stuff off shelves, shouting, running into things, running off and, my favourite, performing some sort of 'show' to their unwilling captive audience.

Yuk. Yuk. Yuk. NO. NO. NO.

Shopping

Shopping is also an errand I suppose but I feel it deserves its own section due to its particularly horrendous nature. I used to see it as a leisure activity but now it's more of an endurance test.

Do you remember going shopping before you had kids and the kinds of things you used to do? Calmly walking through the shops, picking up a book to flick through, spritzing on a bit of perfume, holding a dress up to the mirror, gliding up escalators with the breeze blowing through your hair, smelling a nice-looking candle just cos . . . I think it was called browsing?

The ability to browse dies once you have kids and is replaced by panic-buying.

Even if I do get the time and opportunity to go shopping on my own I feel so under pressure to enjoy that time that I actually panic about not enjoying it enough and therefore panic-buy anyway. Humph.

I still prefer it to dragging my two along with me though. Because . . .

My advice is to do it all online. The internet is your friend. It's more than just a friend. It's sanity-saving. It's a fucking lifeline.

Weddings

Children really do make weddings lovely. Unless
you have to bring your own along, in which case
they just ruin them.

Yes they look cute dressed up, yes they look nice in
the photos and yes for a brief moment, running
across the lawn, giggling while the adults enjoy a
glass of fizz, it feels like they have a place there.
But after that NO. Everyone just ends up at cross-
purposes – I want to unwind and catch up with
friends I've not seen in years, my kids want to try
and take mouthfuls out of the wedding cake and shout
inappropriate things at inappropriate moments.

We had to have children at our wedding, largely because we got married after the birth of Big Bro and we could hardly not invite our own child (could we?!). All I know is that I love when I get invited to weddings and they say 'Sorry no children' because then I know everyone (myself included) is going to have a lot more fun.

The only mistake you might be in danger of making when omitting children from your guest list is that parents on a rare night out, plied with free booze, cannot be expected to behave any better than their kids would have.

Just trying to go for a bloody wee

Need I say more?!

Visiting childless friends

We touched on childless friends on page 61. Great people to visit, just not with children. Children start destroying the houses of childless people because there is nothing else to do. Childless people tend to not like having their houses destroyed because it is scary for them.

Everyone just wants to go to the pub and it just all ends up feeling a bit awkward. Leave the kids with a babysitter and go do shots. The end.

Eating out

I'm not really a tattoo fan. I have a terrible Disney one on my arse that I got in Cornwall on my first girls' holiday aged seventeen. It was bad then and it looks even worse nearly twenty years on (yes I did feel a bit sick when I worked that out) but I kind of like it because it reminds me of a time when I was young and free to empty the contents of my stomach in public doorways. But I digress. If I was a tattoo fan I should probably get one saying 'Eating out with your kids is the most horrific way you could possibly think of to spend £50'.

Hopefully it would prevent me making the same mistake again, every few months, when my mind has blocked the worst parts out.

The problem I find with eating out is that the food is way too colourful (ergo suspicious), it takes too long to arrive (resulting in the unpopular activity of extended sitting) and if you down your babychino in one, and lob the cup over your shoulder unashamedly, well it turns out some places are not quite so *'baby friendly'* after all.

Public transport

No escaping their happy, happy rude chat here is there? My kids always seem to use the time on buses or trains to pick out a poor unsuspecting person and then lean in close to my ear, in an attempt to whisper, but then actually just shout into my eardrum . . .

AT A PERSON WHO IS QUITE CLEARLY A WOMAN!

NOW AND THEN

I had a great childhood. I'm not quite sure, apart from the basics, how my soul fell into my body and was born to my parents but I was bloody lucky that I got them.

If you were to ask me about it (I know you haven't but shhh this is my book!) my mind would automatically swing back to days spent on Worthing beach messing about on lilos in the sea and hunting for crabs in the rock pools; or playing outside with my sisters and other kids from the street, riding about on our bikes and coming home reluctantly as dusk fell.

My mum was always there for us, making toast and snacks, but I don't remember her frantically finding stuff for us to do. We played board games or loaded up Ghostbusters on the Atari. We spent our 20p pocket money on sweets at the newsagents. We bought sherbet DipDabs and Tic Tacs and imagined they were drugs that gave us magical powers. We'd smoke packets of sweet cigarettes because we thought it looked cool. I wrote stories and played with My Little Ponies. I had the pink Dream Castle. Life was good.

My dad had the traditional, hardworking father role. He gave me my first taste of G&T aged eight (I spat it out back then) and he still mixes the best ones today. He will admit the best bit of parenting was when we turned eighteen and were finally able to buy him a pint in the pub.

I decided to ask my mum and dad a bit about what it was like for them when they first became parents in the late seventies and eighties, so I pretended I was Louis Theroux and interviewed them over my mum's speciality boeuf bourguignon . . .

Me: Do you remember what it was like coming home
with a new baby?
Mum: Panic stations. Absolute panic.
Dad: Oh God, well it was awful.

[Cheers Dad!]

Mum: Both you and Caroline [my oldest sister]
were born in January so it was freezing and
snowing and we had no clue what to do. We had no
central heating so Dad lit a fire and we put you
to bed in mittens and a woolly hat.
Dad: Both of our mums were miles away so we had no
help there.
Mum: And we didn't even have a phone. I remember
running up the road to call Mum because Caroline
wouldn't stop crying.
Dad: It makes it sound Victorian doesn't it? It
wasn't far off. It just shows you that kids
survive without all the fancy kit.
Me: What were the hardest bits of parenting do you
think?
Mum: Terry towelling nappies. We had buckets of
dirty nappies in the kitchen, bedroom and living
room.
Dad: The whole house smelt of Napisan. It
absolutely stank.
Mum: We were always washing and drying them in
front of the fire. They had great big nappy pins.

Can you imagine trying to get the pins in with a
wriggling baby?

Me: No, it's hard enough getting a disposable on!

Mum: The liquid poo would just shoot right out.
You got very sore bottoms. Oh and the
breastfeeding advice was to feed every four
hours. I just ignored that. Can you imagine
trying to feed a brand new baby every four
hours?

Me: No, they feed constantly at first.

Mum: Feeding out and about was a big no-no too.
It just didn't happen, you never saw it. I had
to go home or into Mothercare to feed you all.

Dad: But it wasn't that bad, it wasn't that hard . . .
Mum: You weren't even there most of the time!

[Laughter]

Mum: You were at work. I read some books and
    thought I'd be fine but it wasn't as easy as it
    sounded. We had no family around so I started
    going to playgroups to meet people.
Dad: Well there was no internet, no one to connect
    to online so that was the only option.
Me: What about dads generally, were they not
    expected to help as much?
Dad: [looking sheepish] I didn't do anything.
Mum: He didn't change nappies that's for sure!

[They have a debate as to whether my dad ever
    changed a nappy. Conclusion, maybe a few]

Mum: I think generally dads seem to be a lot more
    involved these days don't they?
Dad: My only contribution to parenting was taking
    the TV aerial away when you were naughty. [My
    dad used to take it to work in his briefcase and
    it was the worst punishment ever because
    Neighbours and Home and Away were my life.]
Mum: You did used to walk the streets with them
    in the pram to get them to sleep.
Dad: [looking pleased] Yes. Yes I did do that.

Me: What else was different?
Mum: Well there were no car seats!
Me: Oh blimey I remember losing sleep over travel systems.
Mum: What's a travel system?

[I explain what a travel system is]

Dad: [scoffing] We just put the top of the pram on the back seat. That was our travel system!

Mum: It sounds awful now, you wouldn't dare do that would you? And smoking, Dad was puffing away around you all.

[Cue laughter from the pair of them]

Me: So what did you do to entertain us?

Mum: Well we had no holidays, we never went away did we Michael? No one did. Well Penny and Derek had a caravan but that was about as exotic as it got. We just made sandwiches and took you down to the beach.

Me: It was always hot from what I remember, we went to the beach every day in the summer didn't we?

Mum: Well we did go to the beach nearly every day but it wasn't always hot.

Dad: It was always hot when I was young too. I don't think it rained until I was thirty!

Me: What else did we do?

Mum: Well everything is catered for kids now isn't it? It wasn't when you were young.

Dad: You couldn't go to the pub with kids could you Sue? I remember walking around for ages trying to find a pub that would take kids. That's one thing you have much better now! Kids were meant to be seen and not heard then.

[More laughter]

Me: We used to play out a lot more though too didn't we?

Mum: Yep, well there was nothing to keep you

inside so you were always out, it never crossed our minds that anything would happen to you. It just felt safe.

Now... Then...

Me: Did you work when we were little Mum?
Mum: Yes, most people had jobs of sorts but I just did work to fit in around you girls. I made earrings, sold dried flowers at markets and I did agency nursing at nights when you were sleeping.
Me: What did you do for childcare?
Mum: Well there were no nurseries then and nothing at all for under-threes. You just asked friends, it was more of a community I guess but

with no family around we didn't get much time
for ourselves.

Dad: I remember when Emily [my youngest sister]
started school I took the day off. We went to a
tapas bar, it was our first taste of freedom for
years. We had a bottle of wine and then we went
to pick you all up.

[Laughter]

Me: Do you think kids are spoilt now? Mine never
seem to have enough toys, they always think
everyone else has better stuff.

Mum: You had a lot of toys too but then again
everyone just had the same sort of things. Kids
seem to go through a lot of phases these days
because there is so much more choice. We never
used to spend anywhere near as much money.

Me: Birthday parties are another thing that have
become more and more extravagant, people spend
hundreds on them.

Mum: We always had parties but they were usually
at home. We just made a pass the parcel and
wrapped it in newspaper. I always made the cakes
and we had cheese and pineapple hedgehogs and
crisps. It was much lower key.

Dad: I think kids probably used to enjoy the
naffness of it all even more.

Me: I remember having a McDonald's party once and

getting a kitchen tour! And I always remember
the disco that we had and Dad made the lights by
screwing four coloured lightbulbs to a plank of
wood!

[Laughter]

Dad: Ooh I'd forgotten about that! I did. You
   loved it at the time.
Me: It felt like the height of sophistication!
Me: What about food, did you worry about what we
   were eating?
Mum: Well you were the fussiest. I remember
   making three separate meals because you all
   liked different stuff.
Me: That's why I try not to worry about my boys
   too much because I think they can't be as bad as
   me. [I didn't eat any vegetables at all bar
   potato until I was about twenty-five.]
Me: What do you think of these?

[I show my mum a picture of some of those amazing
   bento box lunches some parents do for their
   kids.]

Mum: Oh my gosh! Those are amazing.
Me: I think healthy eating is a bigger deal now.
   It's a good thing but sometimes it feels a bit
   unrealistic.

Mum: Well yes, you just had the exact same thing every day!

Now...

Animal face sandwiches

Organic Goji berries

Moon and stars veg

Homemade houmous

Sculpted Babybel

Then...

Cheese sandwich

Crisps

Chocolate bar

Me: Did you ever feel judged by other parents or under pressure to do things a certain way?
Mum: No. It wasn't the same, there was no media, no celebrities, no internet forums. There was no perfect lifestyle to live up to. It's all commercialised now. We just used to get on with it, everyone was in the same boat. Everyone had hand-me-downs and the bog-standard basic gear.
Dad: But babies were obviously the same, we just didn't have all of 'the things'. In some ways I think it was a lot easier back then without all

of the distractions. There must be a lot of pressure on parents these days.

Me: Yeh you're right. I think there is.

I think we can learn a lot from our own childhoods: firstly, about what children really 'need' – of course I'm not saying don't bother to get a car seat, but a lot of the fancy gadgets and toys really aren't that necessary. Ditto exotic holidays and expensive day trips; kids don't seem to see the difference between Margate and the Maldives and 95% of the time my boys just want to go to our local park. In fact Big Bro said this to me recently:

'Remember that time when I got that big stick and it was really tall and I carried it ALL day and I got SO tired that I nearly died. But I didn't die. Wasn't it the BEST DAY EVER?!'

I have no recollection of this particular day; however, I can remember wanting to punch myself in the face after spending a fortune just to watch my children cry in the merry hellhole that is Peppa Pig World.

Lesson: If you can't afford it, don't sweat it.

Secondly, I ate a lot of Bernard Matthews Turkey Burgers and Angel Delight growing up and I'm not dead (yet). You'll be happy to know that despite being horrendously fussy as a child I now enjoy a wider repertoire of food.

Finally, it's also OK, or even good, to ignore your kids occasionally. Big Bro will constantly say 'THERE'S NOTHING TO DO!' in a house that more closely resembles a fricking toyshop! Sometimes I can't or just don't want to play with him so I politely but firmly tell him that 'Mummy is busy right now'; eventually he will take himself off and build something cool out of the Lego he just branded 'SOOOOOO BORING'.

It's good for kids to be able to entertain themselves and use their own imaginations. In the real world people get ignored all the time so lavishing attention on kids 24/7 is doing them a disservice right?

I'm hoping this approach will result in mine growing up to be self-sufficient human beings rather than lifelong members of The Special Snowflakes Club.

THE QUEEN OF EMPTY THREATS

There are things we excel at in our house (dancing about the kitchen, devouring jam on toast, farting) and there are things that we are altogether less good at (most things apart from the aforementioned).

Basically stuff done voluntarily must meet the criteria of being funny, fun or delicious, which causes no end of problems with the practicalities of getting to school/nursery/work on time because getting dressed falls into none of those categories. Of course we could make it easier on ourselves by orchestrating the whole process but like many parents we are trying hard to instil some form of responsibility into Big Bro:

So the new house rules are:

1. Before you come downstairs for breakfast you must have put your clothes on by yourself. Claiming that you can't do it is wholly contradictory to, er, YESTERDAY when you did actually do it by yourself, albeit over a forty-five-minute period of pure unadulterated hell.

2. You have to apply your own shoes to your own feet before you leave the house. Poking one toe in one shoe and then proclaiming that you can't do it DOES NOT COUNT as a good effort.

3. Going to the toilet before you piss yourself will also be looked upon positively.

I'm disappointed to say that the improvement has been minimal. Probably because the chosen method of aiding cooperation involves making ridiculous threats and never following through. Sorry Supernanny, my bad.

When I got to thinking about it I realised that nearly everything that comes out of my mouth is absolute rubbish! In fact by the end of the day I often feel like I have exhausted a full arsenal of empty threats including:

Threat – *'If you don't put your shoes on now then you can stay here on your own!'*
Problem – Destruction of the house, destruction of himself. Also, um, illegal.

Threat – *'No more TV/iPad!'*
Problem – I might as well shoot myself in the face, TV/iPad time is the only way I ever get anything done.

Threat – *'If you don't put your toys away I will give them to the charity shop!'*
Problem – Tempting. But in reality I am too weak and scared of my own kids.

Threat – *'If you don't stop that then we are going to leave Krazee Katz Bouncy Barn of Doom right now!'*
Problem – I've just paid a £10 entry fee and ordered a latte.

Threat – *'I'm going to phone Daniel's mum and tell her they can't come round later!'*

Problem – Daniel's mum talks about things other than Batman. I want that.

Threat – *'You won't be going to Sainsbury's if you keep that up!'*
Problem – A very poorly thought-out consequence.

Threat – *'If you don't come now then you can get home on your own.'*
Problem – Cars and baddies. Probable death. A prison sentence for child abandonment.

Threat – *'OK well we won't be going on holiday now.'*
Problem – I am not prepared to lose hundreds of pounds because a toothbrush was lobbed out of the bathroom window.

Threat – *'Stop messing around or you will be walking instead of scooting!'*
Problem – The journey takes five times as long on foot and is peppered with crying and flailing about on the pavement.

Threat – *'Right I'm going to throw your dinner in the bin!'*
Problem – I just spent an hour making it. Instead I'm just going to stare at it lamenting its demise.

Threat – *'Would you like me to tell Mrs Jeffries that when we go to school tomorrow?'*
Problem – We would both look pretty pathetic.

Threat – *'Do you want me to give your teddy* (AKA favourite comforter) *away?'*
Problem – Way too mean. Also makes me feel like a total bitch.

Threat – *'I'm going to count to three and then I'm going to . . .'*
Problem – Do nothing. I'm going to do absolutely nothing.

So where are all of these threats getting me? Nowhere. There is no point in threats that you don't follow through on. I know this but I am only human. When under pressure to get out of the house words fly out of my mouth without checking with my brain first.

So we decided instead of focusing on the negative perhaps we need to concentrate on the positive. Reward charts, people tell me, can work wonders.

Reward charts seem to be one of those opinion-dividing things – some people swear by them, others don't like the idea of having to bribe a child to behave. I'm of the opinion that I don't really care why the child is cooperating as long as they are (with the exception of hitting) and I'm also of the opinion that most things in life are worth having a bash at (with the exception of heroin).

So as reward charts don't commonly involve either of those things and supposedly MAKE BEHAVING FUN we got stuck in.

When it came to drawing up a chart we did consider a simple two-pronged approach:

 You can do it!

	Mon	Tue	Wed	Thur	Fri	Sat	Sun
Not pissing yourself							
Not being a dick							

But although this seemed to cover all the bases, we reasoned it ought to be a bit more specific rather than homing in on the overall personality type. So along with the aforementioned getting dressed rules we added:

- Being kind to your brother
- Eating your meals nicely
- Staying in your bed
- NOT CRYING ALL THE TIME ABOUT ABSOLUTELY NOTHING

We decided that a small reward would be distributed for a full day of stickers (choosing something from the treat tub) and a bigger reward would be distributed for an almost full week of stickers (the much coveted Optimus Prime).

Simple enough right?

Wrong . . .

I explained that throwing half of your dinner on the floor doesn't count and that he would get Optimus Prime at the end of the week IF he got enough stickers, but it didn't go down very well because a week is 'FOREVER!'

It seems we are still stuck in the annoying stage of not being able to talk about anything even vaguely appealing if it is not happening THAT EXACT SECOND.

So I was stuck repeating myself twenty times a day, defining the terms and conditions of the reward chart while simultaneously picking stickers off every goddam surface in my entire house. If you happen to see a destitute blonde woman wandering around Brighton with Batman characters emblazoned across her arse it is probably me. Please don't be afraid to come over and pull them off. I will probably hug you for it.

All in all the verdict thus far is that I hate reward charts, maybe even more than I hate kids in possession of stickers. One of the worst things about them is that they force you to come to terms with your own pathetic failings, i.e. after receiving about 25% of the stickers on his chart . . .

Perhaps we might benefit from having a reward chart as well.

	Mon	Tue	Wed	Thur	Fri	Sat	Sun
Having a backbone							
Not being a dick							
Not looking up kids party themes on Pinterest	★	★	★		NOOO!!!		

And while we are being honest I should also admit that last week we had a birthday cake, complete with candles, even though it was nobody's birthday, because my children are the boss of me.

So as you see I'm not perfect, I can be weak, but we muddle through as best we can and I am still confident that I am raising my kids well despite my misgivings. They are cheeky but polite and a little bit feral but caring.

In an ideal world my kids would do as they were asked and I would always keep my cool. But I'm not built that way, my patience is a little on the low side and there are only so many times I can tolerate 'But what's your favourite *Star Wars* ship Mummy?' type questions in response to 'Could you please brush your teeth?' – before I start losing the will to live.

But there is one thing that always works . . .

Biscuits!

If I was ever going to write a proper parenting manual this would be the one . . .

The only parenting book you'll ever need!

Are you finding it difficult to control a wilful child? Are you fed up with buying parenting book after parenting book and still feeling like an utter twat? Would you like to bitch-slap Supernanny into the middle of next week?

Then why not try . . .

Parenting With Biscuits! It promises you happy, compliant and flexible children with a simple 'Just Add Biscuits' (#JAB) approach.

- Won't let you brush their hair? #JAB
- Feeling too sick to go to school? #JAB
- Refusing to get in the buggy/car? #JAB

- Doing a wee wee dance but saying they don't need the toilet? #JAB
- Repeatedly singing 'Let it Go' in a skin-crawlingly annoying voice? #JAB

Still a little confused? Don't worry, the world is made up of people with varying intelligence levels. We answer your stupid FAQs here:

Q: My kids whine all the time and it does my head in. What should I do?
A: Stick biscuits in their gobs.

Q: My daughter won't eat her vegetables.
A: Yes, because they are not biscuits. Try biscuits!

Q: My son says he doesn't like school any more . . .

A: I bet he likes biscuits though! Think about it . . .

Q: Your method works great until the inevitable sugar crash . . .

A: This only happens if you stop giving biscuits.

Q: What is the best method for dealing with tantrums?

A: Stand well back and repeatedly hurl chocolate Hobnobs until everything goes silent.

Q: Have you ever considered that bribing children into submission is just a temporary fix? I like my kids to behave because they know it's the right thing to do!

A: Fuck off you smug bastard.

Q: What if—?

A: Biscuits

Q: Should I—?

A: Yes. Biscuits.

Q: But—

A: What part of this are you not getting you daft bint?! JUST ADD BISCUITS.

Reader reviews:

'I was really struggling getting my son to put his shoes on in the morning, nothing I tried worked. Then a friend suggested I read Parenting With Biscuits *and it's like he's a different person! These days we are out the door before I've even had chance to say 'custard cream!'*

'Revolutionary – best book I've ever bought!'

'Such an inspiring read. I feel the author has really broken the boundaries of parenting literature with this practical and easy-to-action guide.'

'I can't even begin to explain what a difference a packet of bourbons has made to our family. Thank you so much!'

'So simple you'll wonder why you even needed to buy a book on the subject (but obviously you should still buy the book).'

'Just. Bloody. Amazing.'

Parenting With Biscuits is available from all crappy bookshops now!

Also by the same author:

Be A Better You: With Gin!

Bacon... The Relationship Fixer!

JUST LET GO

Before we have children we often have preconceived ideas about the type of parents we think we will be. Do you know what one of mine was? That I would sit playing the piano while my kids danced and sang around me. I would be a fun, slightly crazy, spontaneous mum and life would always be full of joy and laughter.

This fantasy was ridiculous and unachievable on many levels; firstly I never learnt to play the piano and secondly I doubt we will ever have a house large enough for one anyway. We occasionally have kitchen discos to Taylor Swift when they are not fighting over the bit of plastic tat that is currently flavour of the week, but I'm not sure if that counts?

All I know is that I wanted to be like Julie Andrews but ended up feeling more like Cinderella.

Parenthood Imagined

Parenthood Actual

The main problem with these preconceived ideas or ideals is that they are everywhere. They rear their heads in pregnancy and follow us through to birth and beyond. Earth mother Cass wanted to breastfeed for two years but was mixing up formula after two weeks, hypnobirth Sally ended up with an emergency C-section and 'I only like wooden toys' Sam just bought his toddler her own iPad so he could get five minutes to drink his bastard coffee in peace.

Some of these choices didn't end up being choices at all and others were made for sanity's sake, but do you know what? All of them are just FINE.

But often it's hard for us to see that because it's not just your own internal expectations that are the problem, it's other people's. So we get protective, and the guilt rises up inside us as an angry little ball of words that come out of our mouths as competitiveness, whereby we start justifying our decisions as the right ones, the best ones. We start trying to make ourselves feel better by making other people feel like they are failing.

I'm sure we've all done it to some extent, sometimes without even realising. But if you stop and think, there are no right answers. Every parent feels criticised in their own way . . .

Bottle-feeding mums didn't try hard enough, breastfeeding mums should keep covered up, working mums care more about exotic holidays and fancy cars while stay-at-home mums are just layabouts keeping the local coffee shops in business. Sleep training is cruel even if you are close to breaking point and dummies might provide comfort but have you thought about the potential for speech delay and crooked teeth?

The occasional Happy Meal will make your children obese and putting love-heart-shaped bits of carrot into school packed lunches is just plain showing off. TV might be educational, but it is also evil and those crafty mums who say they do it for their kids really just want people with a glitter aversion to feel bad. Mums who do the school run in no make-up and dirty leggings need to make a bloody effort but that bitch with immaculate highlights in the gym gear – well she deserves to fucking die.

So who is winning? Which one of the above mums (or dads) makes the best parent? Let me tell you this . . . no one is winning. Not if we all keep judging each other.

The only ones who can provide a definitive answer are not the other parents but the ones who you are actually parenting. I decided to continue with my Louis Theroux investigative journalism by asking my sons a bit about what they think makes a good parent . . .

[Interview conducted in the bath to ensure interviewees' full(ish) attention and inability to easily escape.]

Me: Do you think Mummy is a good mummy?

Big Bro: Yes you are the best mummy!

Me: Ahh thank you! You are the best boys. Why do you think I'm a good mummy?

Big Bro: You love me and you give me good cuddles.

Little Bro: You've got a face!

Big Bro: I like your face and your shiny yellow hair.

Little Bro: I like your lellow hair too.

Me: Thank you!

Big Bro: And I like you because you give me strawberry milk on Fridays as a treat and I like it when you buy me Lego. Can you get me the Lego Millennium Falcon?

Me: No.

[Interview terminated because I don't enjoy having discussions about the Lego Millennium Falcon. It's £100. It's not happening!]

I then compared their list to my own and the disparity was amazing!

What makes a good parent?

According to me...

1, Patient
2, Likes crafting
3, Doesn't sigh all the time
4, On the PTA
5, Doesn't pretend to
need a poo so can
lock self in the toilet

According to my boys...

1, Loves me
2, Gives good cuddles
3, Got a face
4, Has shiny lellow hair
5, Makes strawberry milk
on Fridays
6, Buys Lego

So there we go. While I was worrying that my glitter phobia was tarnishing their childhoods, I never knew that 17% of the reason my children view me favourably as their mum is JUST BECAUSE I HAVE A FACE!

So it seems that parenthood is not about always getting things right. It's about muddling through as best as you can and realising that if your kids are warm, fed, loved and happy(ish) then you are not letting them down.

If it's raining outside and you are all going stir crazy they are not going to spontaneously combust if you stick a film on to calm them down. Did you forget last weekend when you spent hours trailing around botanical gardens and stopping them pulling the heads off fancy flowers?

Seriously, how messed up are your kids really going to be because they sometimes caught you looking at your phone instead of pretending to eat the carrot and egg soup they just served you in a plastic teapot?

Welcome to RETFMTS
(Ridiculously expensive therapy for moderately troubled souls)

It's OK to find it boring sometimes. It's OK to get it wrong.

I am never going to make my own Play-Doh or plan World Book Day outfits weeks in advance, my kids would choose chicken nuggets over home-made dinners every time, I am a bit too . . . shouty. Instead of selecting actual outfits I just sniff-test trousers for wee and pick encrusted yoghurt off T-shirts, school projects are always done last minute while swearing into a double G&T, I give in to whining too easily and sometimes I buy them treats they don't deserve because I'm a sucker for a smiley face.

But we also bake the occasional cake, I blitz vegetables into their meals, I fill up the paddling pool in the summer and I squirt them with water from the hose, we go to the beach (a lot) and throw stones in the sea, I laugh at their rubbish jokes, I build train tracks, I talk in-depth about subjects that I have absolutely no interest in and I play out my role of Wonder Woman or Han Solo with as much enthusiasm as I can muster.

Overall I think I'm doing an OK job so why do I keep beating myself up? Why as parents are we always feeling guilty? The only thing we should be feeling guilty about is how guilty we are feeling. Because the guilt only seeks to mar our experiences of parenthood, distract us from our children and pit us against one another. But it's not a competition, there are no prizes or fancy trophies. So if things don't turn out the way you imagined don't let it leave you feeling cheated, don't let it eat you up, don't look at everyone else and think they are doing a better job.

Just. Let. Go.

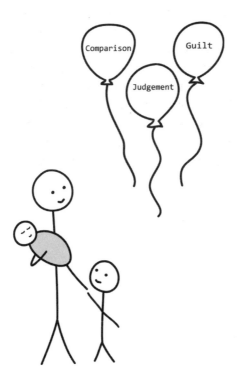

Concentrate on the only ones who truly matter, because they love you just the way you are (warts and all).

STARTING SCHOOL —
WHAT'S THE DEAL?

OK OK, of course I missed him. I'm not that much of a cow!

As we said our goodbyes on that very first day I succumbed to the typical stereotype of sobbing parent with the best of 'em. Perhaps slightly more so because Big Bro was the very youngest in his class . . . not quite so big really at all. In fact he looked pretty damn small standing there, swamped in his uniform against that great big building.

I worried that he wouldn't be able to sit still, that he would feel a little lost without me and that it might all be too much for him. I had a lot of confidence in him you see. But the reality is that I was wrong. He skips through the door happily each day, he condemns people who end up on the 'bad behaviour cloud' and tells me (YES ME!!) off because *'You're not doing good listening Mummy!'*

I was right about one thing, however, and that was that he might not be able to wipe his own bum properly – the skid marks are there to prove it. Hurrah, go me!

Another thing I noticed is that he is ever so slightly more tired than usual. But not in a sleeps longer and takes a nap type way, but as a sleeps less and acts like a rabid dog type way. So there we go. FML. Again.

Normal people tired...   Small child tired...

Oh dear I'm feeling tired I might go have a nice lie down.

Oh dear I'm feeling tired I might go destroy things and make other people cry.

And now this is the bit where I was hoping to talk about the one overriding bonus of school. No not the fact that they are helping to shape my son into an intelligent and well-rounded young man – yes there's that, of course there's that. But I'm talking about the bit that would provide me with a bit of free childcare. I know we are not really meant to call it that, but there are similarities as in I have fewer children on my hands and more money so . . . does what it says on the tin right?

But the reality is that it doesn't feel like much of a break because I feel utterly lambasted by the quantities of admin and requests that are being fired at me on a daily basis. I have been so busy bringing in non-perishable foodstuffs, unsuccessfully ironing on 'easy' iron-on name tags and panicking about getting tickets for 'The Spooky Disco' that I forgot I even had a life.

Do I have a life?

BEEP BEEP – oh hang on sorry I just got a text, maybe it's one of my friends asking if I want to go out for a drink.

Oh no . . . it's just school AGAIN – apparently they are having cottage pie today instead of the planned menu option in order to celebrate British Potato Day.

Like I give a fuck!

What's the etiquette here? Am I supposed to reply and tell them that I'm having a tin of ravioli?

And what's with all the forms to fill out and hand back by yesterday lest you die? I am sorely tempted to slip this into his book bag tomorrow . . .

Dear school,
Yes to all things
bar maiming!
Thank you.

Then there are the infestations to think about.
At least 50% of the time you go to collect your
child there will be a poster up to inform you
that there is a case of nits in the class.
Sometimes there will be a poster to inform you
that there is a case of worms in your class. If
you are super lucky there will be two posters up,
side by side, to let you know that there are both
nits and worms in the class at the same time.
Kids are gross.

Do you know what else is gross? Accepting that
'playdate' will become part of your everyday
vocabulary.

And so we come to the biggest problem with school – having to be there every day. On time. Not in your pyjamas. In the before-school times I used to sort of enjoy our lazy mornings pootling about in our pants before deciding what to do for the day. Now that we all have to wear actual clothes things seem to have gone downhill.

This is basically what happens in our house every morning at 8.30 a.m. . . .

Me: Come on we need to go now or we'll be late!

Big Bro: Do you want to be the pink ranger Mummy?

Me: No I want you to get your coat on.

Big Bro: I'm RED RANGER Let's go SUPER MEGAFORCE MODE! HIIIIIYAH!!

Little Bro: Ooh I do this Mummy! [Squeezes an entire bottle of shampoo on to the carpet]

Me: [Barely audible whisper] For fuck's sake.

Big Bro: [Empties entire crate of Lego on to the carpet] Ooops.

Me: [Audible angry voice, not condonable] For fuck's sake!

Little Bro: Fuck's sake!

Me: Ducks! I said ducks. I was talking about ducks.

Big Bro: Why are you talking about ducks Mummy?

Me: I just like ducks OK. Pick all of that Lego up now please!

Big Bro: No you can just do it when I'm at school.

[He's right I will]

Me: Right Little Bro it's time to get in the buggy.

Little Bro: No I is walkin.

Me: You can't walk we're late. Get in now please.

[I pick him up and try to manhandle him into the buggy while he goes rigid and tries to headbutt me]

Me: BIG BRO, COAT!

Big Bro: Actually Mummy I can't go to school because I'm so poorly. I can't move my leg or walk or anything.

Me: What's wrong with your leg? It looked fine a second ago.

Big Bro: I have a really, really bad cut on my knee – look.

Me: Hmmm can't see anything.
Big Bro: You need to look REAL close. OWWWWWWWW.

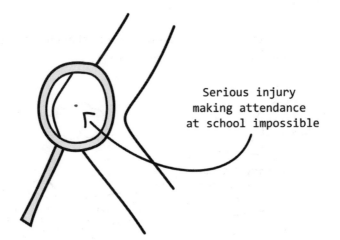

Serious injury
making attendance
at school impossible

Me: COAT! [opens door] We are leaving now.
Little Bro: Oooh is startin rainin Mummy!

ARGHHH he's right! The school run has decided to
rain on us in such a timely fashion that it seems
highly probable that it is doing it ON PURPOSE.

Why d'ya gotta rain on us at exactly drop-off time
and pick-up time?! Are you out to get us SCHOOL
RUN?! Huh?! Huh?! ANSWER ME!

The school run is not an actual person, I do know that. It's just that sometimes the morning routine leaves me feeling a tiny bit unhinged. I hope you understand.

(I sort of wish it was a real person though as I'd really like to kick it in the shins).

OK so school is a lot more work than I thought. But what about the learning? What do they actually do all day? Well. For the most part, I have absolutely no idea because when asked Big Bro responds with 'Nothing' or 'Can I have a snack?', which doesn't sound much like the national curriculum to me (which is a shame as doing nothing and snacking are two of my very favourite pastimes as well). One of the longest conversations I've ever had with him about an event that happened at school was this:

Me: So did anything exciting happen at school today?
Big Bro: Yes.
Me: (EXCITEDLY) Ooh what?
Big Bro: There was a poo in the playground!
Me: Oh right . . . like a bird poo or something?!
Big Bro: No like a boy poo. A boy did a poo in the playground!

Lovely.

But let's get serious again for a minute because I guess we all have concerns about our children starting school, be that because they are young, shy, easily tired or even advanced in terms of their abilities. I could see Big Bro was happy but how was he getting on academically? When I received his end-of-year report it was of no surprise to me that he hadn't hit the required level for literacy or numeracy – he is young, energetic and has a permanent case of ants in his pants, so it was always going to take time. But I know he will get there, so I read the rest of the report, which told me far more than the top-line scores . . .

'He has a brilliant imagination and the creative capability to turn anything into a game.'
He's engaged.

'He demonstrates good speaking skills and has the confidence to share his knowledge and interests with both children and staff.'
He's confident.

'He loves talking about his interests such as Ninja Turtles and Lightning McQueen and shows great engagement when doing so.'
He's happy.

'He has the ability to take risks when trying new things and is beginning to realise the importance of persistence when learning from his mistakes.'
He's trying.

'He really impresses me when he uses the construction toys to make little cars and

Transformers and describes in detail each part of his model and what the function is.'

They have a class of thirty kids, but his wonderful teachers, they really know him!

'It has been an absolute pleasure to teach him this year. He is one of the politest little boys I have ever met! Thank you and well done!'

My face . . . it's leaking.

He may have been the youngest in his class but none of that seemed to matter. The little preschooler who used to knock about by my knees has blossomed into an independent little know-it-all and I feel prouder than I ever have before.

P.S. If any teachers are reading I just wanted to say THANK YOU for the brilliant job you do, you are amazing! Yet also please could you make the termly craft projects easier or at least acknowledge the parental contribution? It's not that I actually mind but I'm just sick and tired of the kids getting all the credit for OUR handiwork.

THE SEVEN STAGES OF SLEEP DEPRIVATION

What size coffee should I have?

A bit tired

Really fucking tired

I know I have a face
but I can't feel it

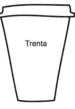

Possibly dead?

So we've talked a lot about sleep already huh? Well it's kind of a big deal to parents so how could we not? But one of the biggest issues is your own sleep and how to cope (or not cope) with the sheer fucking lack of it.

Even if your kids are 'sleepers' (DAMN YOU!) you will still probably be able to relate to this a little because my very, very worst nights, and indeed a few nights of no sleep at all, have been caused by one or both children having the much dreaded D&V bug. Oh the washing, oh the stench, oh the spooning sick off the carpet at 2.30 a.m.

Anyway, you know I don't like to complain so instead I thought I would share my best-practice guide to getting through the day when you are severely sleep-deprived – broken down into easy manageable stages.

Actually maybe it is more of a big long whinge but whatever here we go . . .

1. **Shock** – It's dark, you are toasty warm in bed dreaming of being a world-class gymnast when suddenly there is a small child all up in your face demanding Cheerios, milk and/or a particular toy you haven't seen for months.

   'Go back to sleep,' you say. *'It's the middle of the night!'* you say. But when you reach for your phone to confirm the nonsense hour you see that it is actually morning. Or at least a version of morning, just not a particularly good one . . .

2. **Stalling** – AKA CBeebies or Milkshake!, or a random combination of both because you have perfected the skill of flicking between their very specific programme preferences in your sleep to ensure minimal fuss. If that utter tripe *Cloudbabies* comes on it's game over for everyone.

3. **Denial** – Who needs sleep anyway? You could forgo your plans for the day and stay at home rocking in a corner but that would be weak. Soft play here you come – YOU CAN DO THIS!!

4. **Acceptance** – YOU CAN'T DO THIS! Soft play should be outlawed. Other people's kids should be

outlawed. Your own children need to be made illegal.

5. **Self-Medication** – Have a coffee, have a gin, maybe have a coffee with added gin? Then stuff your face with Tangfastics until you feel sick.

6. **Oblivion** – The coffee-gin-Tangfastic cocktail is not good. Everything is now terrifying. Under no circumstances should you allow your eyes to view even five seconds of *Kate and Mim-Mim*. Her massive purple bunny is no friend of yours.

7. Anger – You are on the home run and start feeling a little triumphant until the inevitable 5.45 p.m. phone call . . .

8. The second wind – Remember how all you've wanted to do all day was lie on the sofa and pass out? Well the kids are finally in bed and guess what?

Now you feel F*CKING AWESOME!

Why go to bed when you have a whole evening to do whatever you like – your lounge is your lobster. You could sit on the sofa half-watching TV and dicking about on your laptop or you could . . . well why think of other options when you could just sit about half-watching TV and dicking about on your laptop?

7.47 p.m. – Perusing Facebook while looking up new cutlery baskets for the dishwasher.

8.23 p.m. – Lasagne and *EastEnders*.

10.01 p.m. – Ooh 30% off at Debenhams ends tonight . . .

11.17 p.m. – Browsing Rightmove for a fantasy house.

11.59 p.m. – A quick Google of teeth-whitening solutions then bed.

9. Insomnia . . .

Fade and repeat.

(*And yes I know there are nine stages rather than seven but I'm sleep-deprived and can't be expected to count accurately.)

DO YOU REMEMBER THE BEFORETIME?

'The beforetime' is how me and J commonly refer to the period of our togetherness before we had kids. It is to be said with an emphasis on the 'before' and accompanied by a knowing, slightly sad, nostalgic look.

We've been together for over ten years now and the story of how we came to be is super romantic. We met at work, we found each other mildly irritating at first but slowly and surely we started to grow on each other. We became friends and I started to realise that I didn't enjoy things as much when he wasn't there.

Then we both got very drunk on a work night out and snogged.

He asked me to be his girlfriend and we filled our time together going out for lunch, laughing, drinking nice wine, mooching about, going to the pub, talking nonsense, mooching about a bit more and going out for dinner. We both liked all the same stuff so it was an easy programme to get behind.

One December a few years later he took me to Tallinn in Estonia and proposed under the big Christmas tree in the main square.

(In the interest of full disclosure, I knew he was going to propose. He had wanted to pick the ring himself but I banned him, knowing full well the exact design I wanted. I dragged him along to Hatton Garden and picked it myself. Call me a control freak if you like because I am one.)

We were giddy, excited and full of love. What a lovely place to be! Little did we know it but at that very moment a small bundle of cells was starting to become a person in my tummy. And that would prove to be the biggest change of all for us.

Fast forward a couple of years and we were married with a toddler. Things were not the same by any stretch of the imagination. We'd gone from a dual-earning 'let's spend all our money going out for dinner three times a week' type couple to a 'who the fuck forgot to buy nappies?' type couple.

I didn't get giddy when I saw him any more. In fact often the sight of his face pissed me off as it reminded me of all the things that had been irritating me about him lately. For example – the way he trims his beard over the sink I've just cleaned and says he's washed it away, but when I go to look there is still hair everywhere! That

sort of thing sometimes makes me feel a bit
stabby . . .

As much as marriage and children can bring couples
together I can quite easily see how it can also
tear them apart. Some separate or divorce, losing
sight of what they ever saw in each other in the
first place, because after kids a lot of it becomes
about the repetitive nature of the daily grind.

We no longer had the ability to get up and say 'Hey
let's go out for brunch' or indeed the ability to
not get up and just spend all day in bed *ahem*.

Instead we would drag our sorry arses downstairs
at stupid o'clock in the morning to referee

breakfast and remove Weetabix from various children's orifices.

Whereas we used to talk about our hopes, our dreams and our crackpot plans for world domination, suddenly now we are talking about Calpol supplies, car seats, remortgaging the house and whose turn it was to put the bins out. Basically life admin. And what's sexy about admin? Nothing. Come to think of it, what's sexy about continuously humming the theme tune to *Paw Patrol?* Yeh – also nothing.

Do you want to know what else is totally unsexy? This . . .

On paper I hate people who do that but in reality - I do that! I ACTUALLY DO THAT! Urgh.

I guess things were hardest when the boys were babies and I was at home and J was at work. I resented his ability to glide out of the door with his headphones on, 'pop' to Pret in his LUNCH BREAK and have actual adult conversations. I'm pretty sure he felt envious of my time with the kids and my not having the financial burden entirely on my shoulders.

When he would return from work and ask simple, friendly questions he would often be met with a *slightly* curt reply . . .

The minor things became the major. Like say, if he didn't order Nespresso pods when he said he would, it would seem like the end of the world. Sometimes it can feel like all my hope for the day lies in those tiny capsules. I've phoned him up at work to give him hell for such misdemeanours and he's told me 'Look I get it, I'm sorry but you need to calm down, I'm working. I'll talk to you later,' with the patience of a fricking saint. (I'm sorry J!)

Mostly we just bicker but occasionally we have ridiculous fights that escalate from nothing. Once he punched the bin lid so hard that it broke and I smashed a wine glass by slamming it into the kitchen worktop (don't worry I had drunk the wine first).

Neither of us are even like that, we are not angry people who can't control our tempers. But children will change you as a couple, the way you think, the way you operate, the things you do, your patience and your sanity levels. Sometimes for the better, sometimes for the worse. It can become increasingly hard to see the person you fell in love with amidst the mounting pile of plastic tat, the laundry, the washing up, the to-do lists and the noisy, demanding small people that you created together.

But we try to grab some time for us among the chaos. Even if it's just falling asleep in front of whatever film we took forty-five minutes to choose on Netflix, even if it's attempting an early night only to have a small child come in at the most inopportune moment . . .

It can be hard, it can be draining, it can all be feeling a bit 'meh' but then something happens and suddenly everything becomes clear again, because for all the work and stress and FML moments that our kids have brought us, they also frequently bring us both to hysterics in a way that only we two could understand.

As they've got older it's got easier; they need less and we are seeing bigger snippets of 'the beforetime' than we used to. It's just a little different these days but if we thought about it properly we wouldn't want to go back (plus it would be impossible anyway so there's no point banging on about it).

So our story is hardly *Romeo and Juliet*, it was certainly never written in the stars but we are still here today, annoying the hell out of each other as always but loving each other regardless.

Here's to many more years sitting mute on the sofa together J! That's about as romantic as it ever gets from me.

'I WILL NEVER LEAVE YOU'

I think all parents at some point have been guilty of wishing the time away. No one could go on taking care of small children forever; it's amazing but relentless, it's rewarding but exhausting, it's utterly spellbinding but it sometimes makes you want to remove your own eyeballs with a spoon.

In my head the holy grail of parenting is the point when my kids will get up and make their own breakfast, put the TV on and leave me in bed to snooze. I'm not there yet but I can see it on the horizon and as time ticks on I know I will get back more and more of what I crave – the ability to sit down for five minutes without someone shouting demands, the time to read a book and drink coffee that I didn't have to microwave four times. One day there will be peace and quiet in a house once buzzing with lightsaber battles and nonsensical toilet-based humour.

But it will be bittersweet of course because while my children are, and always will be, the centre of my world, since the day they were born they have been slowly learning that I am not the centre of theirs.

I watch them swing from milestone to milestone – smiling, clapping, crawling, walking, talking, bike riding, reading, writing and wiping their own squidgy bottoms (or at least trying to). I watch them become more and more independent; with my help they are learning to live a life without me there.

One day in the not-too-distant future I won't be required to do up buttons and soothe scuffed knees with kisses. I won't have to pretend I can't hear the giggles that easily give away hiding places and I won't be pushing cars around on the floor for what seems like hours on end. I won't be needed to help build Lego models and I won't be yelping in pain when I step on the discarded bricks.

One day I won't be wiping sticky jam faces and I won't have to pretend that I like watching *Power Rangers* on TV. I won't be pouring bedtime milk or telling stories and I won't have to lie on the floor of a dark room waiting for my sweet boy to fall asleep. I won't have children hanging off my limbs or wrapped around my body, I'll have an armchair to myself but I'll sit there with the emptiest of empty laps.

One day, when I have all the time in the world, I'll only want to give it back.

Me and Big Bro first had this conversation a while back and it's one we still have frequently now. I'm not quite sure how it started but we were talking about families . . .

'When you grow up you might want to get married like Mummy and Daddy.'

'What? What's married?'

'It's when you find a best friend and you want to live with them and be with them forever.'

Long pause as TINY MIND IS BLOWN, followed by scared look

He gazes up at the ceiling and shakes his head from side to side like he does when he's trying to find the right words in the right order.

'But, but, but, but . . . and not be with you Mummy?'

Christ.

How do you explain the future to a kid who can't see past the end of his elbow and who has only just fathomed the concept of tomorrow?

I open my arms and he links his hands behind my neck and swings his legs round my waist. He's heavy and I wonder if this will be one of the last times I scoop him up like this. Or if this will be one of the last times he will want to be scooped.

I look deep into his confused little eyes and tell him straight.

'You are my best friend and I will never leave you.'

And it's true.

Because I know he will be the one that leaves me.

THINGS (I THINK) I WANT MY KIDS TO KNOW

There are shedloads of lists like this floating around the internet, life lessons so important that people need to write them down on the World Wide Web in case they forget to actually teach them to their kids.

It seems kind of relevant to end with something similar because since I've been writing this book I've been having anxiety dreams about getting killed in a freak accident just before it gets published and therefore never getting to see it in print. I've also imagined the aftermath and some surprisingly positive things actually: the book gets lots of press coverage due to my tragic ending, because everyone loves a bit of morbidity right? The major bonus here is to my family, who are able to buy a better car and go on a posh holiday. I'd like to think it would soften the blow a little.

Anyway enough chat about death, let us get on and finish up with all the stuff I have learnt thus far:

For my boys, this is the stuff you really need to know . . .

I. *The top five best crisps in the world are:*
   1. *Pickled Onion Monster Munch*
   2. *Scampi N' Lemon Nik Naks (really ought to be more widely available)*
   3. *Wotsits*
   4. *Frazzles*
   5. *Flame Grilled Steak McCoy's*

2. *The right way to put the loo roll on is with the flap on the front side and NEVER with it hanging down the back.*

3. *Travelators are there to speed things up not slow them down, ditto escalators. Don't block them up with your suitcases and/or body positioning – it can make people feel VERY CROSS!*

4. Invest in a decent coffee machine because coffee makes things like talking in sentences 'seem' possible.

5. Being cheerful and grateful is nice but it can also be exhausting. Allow yourself to take a break from being nice and enjoy wallowing in your own misery once in a while.

6. When you have had enough of wallowing - try bubble wrap.

7. *Life is too short to be doing things you don't enjoy. Learn how to say no to people. If you find it hard practise on a pet.*

8. *Don't be a round dodger, you might think you are getting away with free drinks but EVERYONE knows.*

9. *I NEVER EVER want to see you on reality TV (unless it's MasterChef).*

10. *There will always be people who are cleverer or more talented than you. If you can't deal with that then try and pick friends who are slightly more rubbish than you or learn to keep bad thoughts inside your head.*

11. However, people who 'think' they are better than you are actually just dicks.

12. Gazpacho is just wrong. Cold soup?! Why, why, why?

13. Tell your friends everything you love about them and look people in the eye when you talk to them . . . but don't stare at them incessantly. Also don't be a stalker, it's creepy and illegal.

14. Don't argue with people on the internet, you will get sucked into a vortex and lose many valuable hours and brain cells.

15. Aspire to be the complete opposite of Gwyneth Paltrow.

This is for you Gwynnie!

16. Your faces are bloody lovely.

17. *Pretty much everything in life can be considered a waste of money but the only surefire way to waste money is dying with a load of cash in the bank that you should have spent on the stuff you never did.*

18. *Don't let people make you feel pathetic for liking stuff that's not highbrow. I have appalling taste in music but a weight has been lifted from my shoulders since I openly declared myself as a Belieber.*

19. *This is the best joke ever . . .*

Q: What's brown and sticky?

A: A stick!

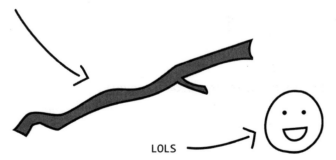

LOLS

20. Shall we do a semi-serious one? I'd love to tell you how special you are but the chances are . . . you are probably not. This whole 'Shine bright my darling!' thing is all well and good but if you try and shine brighter than your allotted wattage you will blow the fuse and leave everyone else around you sitting in the dark. There is a lot to be said for the simple things – a job you don't hate, a person to share your life with, family, a roof over your head, beans on toast for dinner and enough money to buy a good friend a drink. There is a lot to be said for rejecting the draw of grandeur and just enjoying the freedoms that come with being utterly average. There is a lot to be said for being normal, being normal suits most people just fine.

21. Here's another. There is only one world; people might look different, sound different or believe in different stuff to you but deep down we are all the same. Welcome everybody and help those who are less fortunate than you. It sounds simple enough but lots of grown-ups get it wrong – you're the ones who can make things right. Pass it on!

22. I'm sure there are lots of other serious ones I should mention – be nice to animals, vote, recycle, remember to brush your teeth, drive carefully, learn to forgive, eat more kale etc. etc. but I'm getting bored now and Gwyneth eats kale, so meh. OH . . .

23. *Did you know I never laughed so hard before I met you? Can you see how proud you make me every day? Do you realise that you are everything I ever wanted? I love you. Always. With the whole of my heart (imperfect bits and all).*

xxx

ACKNOWLEDGMENTS

Cheers m'dears!

Ahh this is terrible: where does it start? Where does it stop? What if I accidentally forget someone important?! Should I credit my pets?! Who knows but here we go . . .

To everybody who reads, comments and shares my blog - without you this would never have happened so thank you for help making a dream come true and for making me laugh on a daily basis with your fabulous tales of parental woe and wonder.

To the brilliant team at Coronet - Emma, Alice, Rosie and especially my editor Charlotte who noticed me a long while ago before I had many followers (if her boss is reading she needs a promotion for frequently working on my book at 5am!).

To my friends. Oh am I lucky to have so many wonderful ones in my life! And only now when I write this do I realise that they are all categorised into stupid gang names. To THE gang – bang my face, to the People Who Are Not Shit – the voices of reason in this crazy world, to the Lloret 11 – what a holiday that was, I can't even remember not knowing you. To The Foxz – how incredibly arrogant were we? But you know . . . rightly so, and to The West Hove Massive, probably the only group of people capable of making me look like a lightweight.

Special shout outs to Harriet for the free psychotherapy you provided when I fell into a hole of self-doubt mid-way through this book - thank you for pulling me out. To Emma, because ASLAN?! You freak (told you I'd get it in). To Annie and Karen - my spirit animals, to Nathalie – drinking White Russians covered in gloss paint will always be my happy place and to Jane – the day Tony decided to quit uni, my whole life changed for the better.

To my family. Mum and Dad for just being awesome and setting the bar so high, it's great to have parents that feel just like friends. Ditto to my sisters, my wonderful in-laws and my gorgeous nieces and nephews. To Norman and Sheila for welcoming me into your family and all the amazing babysitting you do.

To my little guys, you crazy fools! Thanks for being a constant source of content, I know I've said it already but I love you both to the moon and back and then to the universe and back, and then around the sun one million billion trillion times. You seriously can't top that. I win.

To J, you're alright too I guess ;) *safety wink*. Thank you for being a wonderful husband, daddy and supporter of my drawing stupid pictures on the internet instead of getting a real job. Ta for always forgiving me for being a dick too – you did know that when you married me though.

Finally to Thumper, Thumper (2) and Bumper, Flopsy, Jack, Smokey, Piggy and Pickle – sorry you're all dead now. Hope it's nice up in animal heaven.

FUNNIEST TANTRUMS COMPETITION

Since I began Hurrah for Gin I have been
overwhelmed by comments and messages from people
sharing their own hilarious parenting tales. It
seemed only right to include some of those gems in
this book so we asked you to share your own
TANTRUM HORROR STORIES via the mumsnet bloggers on
facebook because there is nowt funnier than small
people losing the plot for absolutely ridiculous
reasons. We read through hundreds of fabulous
entries but I had to pick just three - these are
my favourites ...

1, From Mark Smith

'I did the 'pull my finger' thing (I'm a dad and therefore it's the law) and let fly a beauty. Daughter (2 yo) copied and I pulled her finger. She totally shat herself and went nuts. Probably too inappropriate to win but still makes me laugh.'

Too inappropriate to win Mark? Never!

2, From Nicola Hardy

'Getting changed, in walks 3 year old. Starts panicking that my boobies are on the floor (I had changed my bra and popped the dirty one on the floor for the wash). Demands I put them back on. Starts screaming and freaking out and telling me to ring doctor brown bear to get them put back on. I explain it's called a bra and it's where my boobies live. Picks it up and throws it away and seems very freaked out over the whole experience!'

Sounds like an extremely traumatic experience Nicola. I hope she's recovering well.

3, From Clair Morris

'First born daughter was about two and up in the night feeling sick. I'm crap during the night so passed her over to husband. He tried to cheer her up by lifting her over his head and as he opened his mouth to talk to her, she puked straight down into his mouth. The worst bit is that he didn't want to freak her out by hurling it back at her so he swallowed it. She freaked anyway and was livid that Daddy stole her sick.'

Ahh bonding at its very finest Clair – good job dad!

ABOUT THE AUTHOR

Katie Kirby is a social media strategist/writer/drawer/ greetings card maker and lives by the sea in Hove with her husband and two young sons. She is 36 years old yet still feels about 19. Unfortunately she looks 36.

She has a first class honours degree in Advertising and Marketing, which she largely attributes to her life skill of bullshitting rather than intelligence or hard work. After spending several years working in London media agencies, which basically involved hanging out in wanky London restaurants and doing even more bullshitting, she had some children.

The children were NOT like the ones you see in Boden catalogues and Katie decided to start a blog about the gross injustice of it all.

Some people liked the blog and said it was funny, other people called her an offensive, foul-mouthed alcoholic who can't even draw. She views all of those things as compliments (apart from the drawing one – rude!).

Anyway blah, blah, blah - she won some awards and wrote a book. It is this book you are holding – magic!

Apparently In this section you might also like to learn more about Katie's personal preferences? No? Tough . . .

Katie likes gin, rabbits, over-thinking things, the smell of launderettes and Monster Munch – this is the fifth time she has now mentioned Monster Munch (6th!) and she wonders if she will be rewarded for her loyalty with a lifetimes supply . . .

She does not like losing at board games or writing about herself in the third person – it makes her feel sick.

hurrahforgin.com
facebook.com/hurrahforgin
instagram/hurrah4gin
ginbunnyprints.com